Las Niñas
A Collection of Childhood Memories

Sarah Rafael García

Floricanto™ Press

Copyright ©2008 by Sarah Rafael García
Copyright ©2008 of this edition by Floricanto™ Press and Berkeley Press.

All rights reserved. No part of this publication may be stored in a retrieval system, transmitted or reproduced in any way, including but not limited to photocopy, photograph, magnetic, laser or other type of record, without prior agreement and written permission of the publisher.

Floricanto is a trademark of Floricanto Press.
Floricanto™ Press
650 Castro Street, 120-331
Mountain View, California 94041
(415) 552-1879
ISBN: 978-1-888205-09-1

Edited by Roberto Cabello-Argandoña and Kerri Krueger

Cover design and illustration: Nydia García Castellanos
Content Editing: Suzanne García Mateus
Author's Photo: Vincent Shay Media

Las Niñas

En memoria de Rafa, Sara y Las Niñas

To my Godson Rafael:

We hope you learn more about us and your Abuelito Rafa through our memories.

Acknowledgements

My sisters and Mami, Sara Elba Bustamante, have helped me write *Las Niñas*. The memories of my father, Rafael Castillo García, have kept *Las Niñas* alive. I have always wanted to write this novel but I never knew how to begin or which memories to share. My first story was written as I sat at a café in Beijing, China in the fall of 2004. My last one was completed one week before submitting the final manuscript to Floricanto Press in the fall of 2007. I escaped my life in America for eighteen months in order to begin my own experiences and write *Las Niñas*. Upon my return to California in the spring of 2006, it took another eighteen months to initiate the publishing process. Without the unconditional support of my sisters, Suzanne García Mateus and Nydia García Castellanos, and my mother's persistence pushing me to do more, I would never have gotten to this point in my life. *Gracias a mis hermanitas y mis padres, sin cuyo amor y apoyo, no podría sobrevivir o disfrutar mis sueños.*

Luz E. Herrera, Lonnie Limón, Yvonne De La Peña and Erdem Ay have been my surrogate agents, advisors, and best friends who have helped me strive for *Las Niñas*. They have been my mentors and biggest fans.

I will always be thankful for my entire family; they have played an important role in my life and in *Las Niñas*, especially my cousins and *mi Abuela* Catalina, *Abuelita* María *y Abuelito* Javier. I owe special gratitude to Yolanda García and James Coan, Frank García, Rubén and Mari Bustamante and Liz and

Javier Bustamante for they have paved the road for our family's future.

The passionate interest of all my friends has been an everlasting source of encouragement. I have received great advice and support throughout the years from Héctor and Denise Arcaya, Gabriel A. Sandoval y Familia, Tammy Jo Kinkead, Ditrick Dunn, Alfonso Valverde, Lia O'Neale, Arlene Burgos and her husband Jorge, Tammie Casale and Family, Isabel Salazar y Familia, Aexis Liester, Alma Ramírez and Jigna Patel. Much love to my brother-in laws, Mario Castellanos and Marcus S. Mateus.

I am also very grateful for all my foreign friends that helped me during my stay in China, Doug Hughes from Virginia, Mike Saunders from NY, Jordan Huruska from Brooklyn, Money Mike, Liz and Marissa from Cali, Teresa Che Hui and her family in Shenyang, Pamela De La Canto from Chile and France, Emil Wong from Tennessee and China, Max, Adriana and Urson from Texas, Peter, Geoff, Jen, and Benn-my great friends from Oz, and Andy from the UK. I also can't go without mentioning all my wonderful students in China who gave me the opportunity to teach them English and made a difference in my life, *Xie, Xie*!

Special appreciation to Danny Nugent from Canberra, Australia, he changed my outlook in life since the moment we met and continues to be a great source of encouragement even when he's on the opposite side of the world. He has always believed my book would get published, and I will forever hold his unbinding friendship close to my heart.

I feel privileged to be part of a Central Coast wine country community which includes Becky and Lowell, Greg M., Bevelina and Tom, Diane Moreno, Stephanie Lo Duca, Kelly Girl, her husband Ron and the girls,

Las Niñas

Jeff Dad and his son Chef Jeff, Rebecca and David, Adrienne Rousse, Jeanette and Tracy, Ray and Shirley, Kim and Robert, Laura, Ken and Becky, Cliff Stepp and all my favorite wine tasters that allowed me to talk to them about my dreams of becoming a published writer. So raise your wine glass, here's a toast to you!

Roberto Cabello-Argandoña with Floricanto Press helped me publish *Las Niñas*. Without his interest *Las Niñas* would not be in your hands now. *¡Muchas Gracias por la oportunidad y la fe en Las Niñas*!

I only hope that I have used the right words to help you understand what all these people have seen in the lives of Sarita, Chuchen, and Nini - *Las Niñas* - our shared memories keep us living.

Sarah García

January 5, 2008

Sarah Rafael García

Table of Contents

Introduction..... 11

Chapter One..... 15
Life ends, Life begins...

Chapter Two..... 21
Hide & Seek

Chapter Three..... 26
Ch-air, ch-air chair!

Chapter Four..... 34
Nuestra Mami

Chapter Five..... 38
¡Patas de Rana! Frog Legs?

Chapter Six..... 43
Abuela Cata y Las Primas

Chapter Seven..... 49
Sacramento or Bust!

Chapter Eight..... 57
Las Tías

Chapter Nine..... 62
Pecos River

Chapter Ten..... 65
Twinkie, La Perra

Chapter Eleven.....		71
Mi Primera y Última Comunión

Chapter Twelve.....		77
Plums, Plums and More Plums!

Chapter Thirteen.....		81
Once upon a bedtime...

Chapter Fourteen.....		85
Alice Monique

Chapter Fifteen.....		92
¡La Gran Fiesta!

Chapter Sixteen.....		98
Noé, my first love.

Chapter Seventeen.....		104
Suzanne & Ballet

Chapter Eighteen.....		112
I hate my life...así puede ser la vida!

Chapter Nineteen.....		116
Um, Nydia? Oh Nini!

Chapter Twenty.....		121
We all start in kindergarten...

Afterword.....		128

Glossary		131
Common Spanish Terms.....

Introduction

For some reason everything seems to be in black and white, I can feel a strong hand guiding me through each step. The happiness I feel is unbearable as I witness an angel-like figure staring at me from a distance. Young and beautiful with long dark hair, she sits on the porch of a rather old wooden house surrounded by trees and flowers. I feel my feet stumbling beneath me, but I'm safe. The warmth from the palm grasping my hand extends to a dark figure lifting me with his strong arms and placing me on the angel's lap. I feel her caressing me and kissing my forehead. I hear sweet whispers from both figures, but I can only understand the feeling of love embracing me. Thirty years later, I recall this illusion and finally acknowledge the experience as the first memory of my parents, *Papi y Mami*.

As unbelievable as it may sound, I have many childhood memories that have captured my attention, sometimes in the middle of the night and other times as I hear similar stories from family and friends. Fond memories have outlined my life and provided me with a better understanding of myself as well as illustrating the importance of those around me. But I can't say anything has made such an impact in my life as sharing my life memories with my childhood best friends, *mis hermanas*, my sisters.

I am the eldest of three daughters. "Sarita" I can still hear the various family members' voices saying my name, but it's only a memory now because with time and transition I have been established as "Sarah." I have hazel eyes that I inherited from both of my grandmothers and a name with a legacy that reminds people of my mother and my maternal great grandmother. Being the first grandchild in the family provided me with many advantages growing up, but also gave me additional responsibilities and expectations that had to be met in the eyes of my parents and society. My sister Suzanne is two years younger than me, but our birthdays are only a week apart. She is known as the funny one and still referred to as "Chuchen" by our Grandfather. She dealt with hand-me-downs and was always referred to as Sarah's sister, which inevitably made her seek additional attention as the middle child. My youngest sister, the prettiest of the three, has always been and will continue to be "Nini." Her birth name is "Nydia," but has never really stuck, at least not among the family. As the youngest, she learned to observe and not over react like her sisters. When she does communicate, she is blunt and direct, making sure that her statements are heard.

Sarita is a common Spanish nickname for someone with the name Sarah or Sara, and means "little Sarah." Chuchen is a nickname derived from the name Susan, or, in this case, Suzanne. Nini is a nickname derived from the name Nydia.

We are often referred as "Las Niñas," (meaning "The Girls") since we are the eldest grandchildren. We are also known as the second generation of the García girls. My father's side of the family was blessed with a house full of rambunctious women. We are the first generation on both sides of the family to be born in the United States. All three of us were born in Brownsville, Texas and raised in Orange County, California. We spent our childhood summers visiting our family in Texas.

Our parents, also referred to as *Papi y Mami* ,

were born in Matamoros, Tamaulipas, Mexico. They arrived in Brownsville, Texas in their early teenage years with their parents and met each other a couple of years later. They were married in 1972 at the ages of twenty-one and seventeen and relocated to Santa Ana, California in 1978. Our grandparents and ancestors originated from the depths of Mexico with traces leading us through the roads of Spain. I have never really done much research, but I have heard countless stories from my grandmothers, and those are the only facts I will ever need to know about who I am. Looking back, I don't think anything can compare to those moments in which my grandmothers shared their vivid memories with me while I enjoyed their authentic homemade tortillas.

The relationships with my sisters are the strongest I have ever had. I can't imagine ever being as devoted to anyone else as I am to them. Sometimes our bond is so great we often forget who experienced what in the past. On several occasions I have listened to one of my sisters sharing the same memory I had once believed was my own personal experience. Until this day we both swear it's our own. I used to think all sisters share the same relationships as we have, but to my astonishment, not everyone has had the pleasure of experiencing such a bond with their siblings.

As "Las Niñas" we have lived through many adventurous and realistic childhood stories, some being more of a twisted comedy, while others depicted the struggles we faced as Mexican-American children assimilating in our family's new country. The stories you are about to read are by no means strictly speaking pure facts; but flamboyant childhood memories. The stories conveyed the experiences I remember, through the eyes of "Las Niñas," and are not in any particular order. The stories take place prior to our father's death and at times, reflect his impact on our lives, ultimately providing a childhood that helped us survive his loss. In any case, the moments we have to share have been experienced with lots of tears, laughs, and an abundance of love. Hopefully, they will provide our children with great memories for the generations to come. Sarita, Chuchen, and Nini consist of fond recollections of a childhood that is continuously being lived in each one of us every day.

Chapter One

Life ends, Life begins...

The church was filled with so many people and I hardly recognized anyone attending. As I looked over to the other pews, I saw familiar faces—friends and both sides of my family gazing at my sisters and me. There were stares of despair that made it seem as if we were the ones resting in the coffin at the altar. Unknowingly, a part of our childhood and future seemed to have had passed away, as well; a part, which we would notice that was gone when a significant event led us to believe that our life would have been different if our father never passed away.

I was thirteen when *Papi* passed away. It broke my heart to acknowledge that my youngest sister, barely ten years old, was experiencing such a loss—three years difference in age felt like an eternity. I felt so obligated to take care of *mis hermanitas.*

My loss was not as enduring as that of Suzanne or Nini, simply because I spent more years with our father than they did. With every year that passed, I reflected on that experience. I guess that's what motivated me to share these memories from so long ago.

The church was filled as far back as I could see from the first pew. People stood up against the walls and huddled at the church doors. Not one of us was crying, and I was still in disbelief and trying to be strong for our mother. Classmates holding candles surrounded us, and some of my father's friends stood nearby, while my mother held us all very close to her.

I found myself staring at the coffin hoping I made the right choice with the color. I was told not to pick one too dark because it would be too depressing. Apparently, my family felt I was grown up enough to pick out a coffin and service cards, but not old enough to drive or have a boyfriend.

Since we lived in California and my father's parents lived in Brownsville, Texas, it was decided that he would be buried at their family's future burial site. Within a blink or two, we were in Brownsville at another service for our father. It seemed less welcoming than the first and felt like the rosary before the burial.

Through the multiple services, the long rosary, and the daunting sprinkles of the dirt, people felt compelled to abide by our Mexican culture and Catholic religion, somehow forgetting that children were involved in the loss. Even to this day, I hold resentment towards my family for making us experience his death three times, as if we needed to have a separate service for each one of us. At the rosary, I met some family members for the first time, and in some cases, the last. It was crowded and very uncomfortable. Some of our family members didn't recognize us or pay their respects to my mother.

It's ironic how you can't remember some things even when you write them down, while other moments are embedded in your memory and are never forgotten. My thoughts were to disappear and find my father. As much as I knew I may have been in denial, I just wanted to see him one last time. I stared out the big window at the entrance of the funeral home. The only item marking its entrance was a rather old mesquite tree. I stared so hard that everything around me became mute. I tuned out the crying and the embracing, and even forgot about my sisters for a moment. I got to see him one last time. He was leaning against the mesquite tree staring back at me. He didn't seem sad or worried, but appeared a little heartbroken and understood he could not do anything about it. Now, I am not sure how the illusion appeared, but whatever the reason, it helped me overcome the days that followed.

Sarah Rafael García

Otro día pasa,

Recuerdo mi Papi descansando al lado de un árbol afuera de su propio velorio. Todos adentro llorando lágrimas y yo sin una gota que derramar.

Lo vi por la ventana a la entrada del edificio que escogimos, el cual representaba su muerte, la muerte de mi Papi.

Familias conocidas y desconocidas pasaban para darme sus besos sin sonrisas y a veces con caras tan largas que me dolía tener que verlos. Me sentía tan mal por ellos.

Unas pocas horas pasaron y mi Papi se quedó descansando bajo de un árbol, observándome y el escenario tan triste que pintamos. Si pudiese cambiar el ambiente lo hubiera hecho. En ese momento me di cuenta que el que extrañábamos era aquél que estaba afuera...el que disfrutaba de la vida, no la muerte, aquél que buscaba el apoyo y amor de su familia, no las lágrimas y tristeza de aquellos que sufren.

Antes de salir del velorio, pasó un carro tocando música, una cumbia, yo creo. En ese momento mi Papi se desapareció bailando. Así lo recuerdo, siempre bailando, después de la vida.[1]

(Footnote)

[1]

Another day passes,

I remember my father resting next to a tree just outside his viewing. Everyone inside is shedding tears and I don't have a single tear to hide.

I saw him through the window, at the entrance of the building that we chose to represent his death, my father's

Las Niñas

death.

Familiar and unfamiliar family members paid their respects with a kiss on the cheek without a smile and at times with such long faces that it hurt me to have to see them. I felt so bad for them.

A car drove by, playing some Spanish music and interrupted my vision. I recognized the tune. It reminded me of the music my dad would dance to at weddings. I looked back at the mesquite tree and saw my father dancing away. That's just how I remember him, dancing after life.

I really don't remember much, but not because of the many years that have passed. I simply can't remember any of the details. After six months went by I asked my mother if we drove or flew to Texas, and neither she nor I could recall the plane ride, but she had the ticket stubs to confirm the trip. After Suzanne read this story, she reminded me that our uncle Rubén drove us back to California after the burial, a part of the event none of us remembered. Suzanne confirmed the clarification after a conversation with our uncle fourteen years after our father's death.

At the burial, I remember a lot of crying and it was all very overwhelming. I am not sure who requested such an inconsolable act, but it was insisted that the coffin be lowered in front of us. I remember being so angry that I envisioned myself screaming, "He is going to come back!" and attempting to run towards the coffin while someone held me back. Unfortunately, I recently found out that I actually did it. I can also firmly recall my mother crying and being harassed by family to sprinkle dirt on my father's coffin. My mother could barely stand, much less see through her tears.

From that day forward it seemed that we not only lost our father, but we lost the fond memories of our family. The life we had prior to my father's death had been protected by him. The life without my father led us to open our eyes and see every person for who they really were rather than who we wanted them to be. In that coffin my father took with him *las niñas y su esposa*, the girls and his wife. No one seems to know that they were burying "Rafael Castillo García y familia"[2]. It was the end of one life but the beginning of our new family, Sara and the girls.

[2] *Rafael Castillo and family*

Chapter Two
Hide & Seek

There are many stories I have prefaced with the statement, "Our parents were very young when they got married and had children," which easily translates to our parents being very naïve and inexperienced. There was a period in our childhood in which we were unsupervised throughout the long summer days. My mother was working at the time, but they still could not afford to pay for a babysitter for all three of us. I was considered old enough at the age eleven, and was given the responsibility of watching over my sisters. It's amazing how creative children can be when you provide them with lots of time and unsupervised access to their home.

One of the major rules we had when left home alone was that we could not go outside unless it was the backyard. My parents used the threat of leaving us with a neighbor to prevent us from walking out the front door. "Hide and Seek" inside the house was among the many games we played to keep busy throughout the day. There are many unique places to hide in our home, but most of the ones we used were probably not the safest.

"Ok, I'll count to 100. Suzanne you hide first, then you Nini. Ok go!" I said excitedly. "One, two, three..." As I counted, I tried to think of all the possible hiding places that existed in our home. I eliminated the obvious locations first, such as under our beds, in bedroom closets, and in the bathrooms. Then I started going through all the places I would hide Nini. Nini was pretty small and slender. She could fit into a lot more places than Suzanne or I. I was too chubby to fit in most of the small areas.

I could never imagine Nini growing up to be who she is now, the tallest of the three of us at the height of 5'6." Many times we were afraid she would break if she fell or bumped into anything. In fact, Suzanne often comically described the dream she had about our little sister breaking into pieces after she shoved her to the ground. She had to tape her back together before our parents caught her in the act.

We would sometimes practice hiding Nini in odd places to see if she would fit. Our favorite location was the clothes hamper. One time Nini got in trouble and was sent to her room. Suzanne and I felt bad for her, so we offered an escape. We decided to hide her in our hamper and carry it to the kitchen so we could all share a coke without our parents finding out. The challenge in this was getting past the living room where they were watching TV. Now, I am pretty sure our parents figured us out long before we crossed their paths, but they seemed to enjoy humoring our efforts as mischievous children.

We placed Nini in the hamper, covered her with our dirty laundry, and then a blanket. Suzanne and I couldn't manage to carry the hamper all the way to the kitchen without dropping it a couple of times. Through deviant giggles we would ask the hamper out loud if it was ok. I'm sure it was awkward enough that we were taking our hamper to the kitchen, but we felt it would be convincing to our parents if we announced to them that we were taking our dirty clothes to the laundry room, a chore that we never actually did.

"98, 99, 100! Ready or not here I come!" I searched a couple of locations to make them think I couldn't hear them scrambling to their hiding places. I opened the blanket closet because Nini had fit in it in the past. I also checked the double door cabinet that was part of the coffee table. Suzanne's favorite place to hide was behind the couch because she liked to scare us by jumping out and lunging towards us. All the usual places were empty, so I listened carefully for any noise I could hear. I heard something coming from the kitchen, which was near the garage. I couldn't think of any place they could hide in the kitchen, so I assumed they were hiding in the big tub of clothing we had in the garage. As I walked through the house I tormented them by announcing my presence so they would make more noise out of nervousness. I couldn't hear a sound. I made my way through the kitchen and heard a door close. I turned towards the garage door and made my way to it slowly.

As I turned the knob, I heard some stumbling. I opened the door only to find Suzanne standing on her tiptoes and reaching over the dryer trying to push a button. I screamed "Aha! Hey! Why aren't you hiding?" She looked at me with a blank stare."What are you doing? Where's Nini?" I asked, puzzled. She looked at the dryer and said, "I just wanted to see if she would fit in there and she said she could breath, she said I could turn it on, I asked her..." Not knowing how to react, I yelled at Nini to get out. Nini pushed on the door and said, "I can't open it, its black in here!" I opened the dryer door only to find Nini curled into the small space with her little eyes twinkling back at me.

"Get out Nini! Suzanne you are going to be in so much trouble! Nini could have died if you turned it on!" Suzanne immediately started crying while Nini shyly climbed out of the dryer.

"Don't say that! She wouldn't die!" Suzanne cried out loud.

"She might have broken something!" I stated with

my hands on my hips. Soon after, while eating flour tortillas with butter for lunch and drinking apple juice, we agreed not to tell our parents so they would continue to leave us home alone.

Throughout the years, many of our family members have said that our bond is so great because we had to make do without our father at such a young age. To tell you the truth, I don't think that's the real reason. *Papi*'s death definitely made us stick close together, but I can't say it's the foundation of our bond. No it's our family life that created our bond, not our father's death. Both of my parents thrived on establishing the importance of family, especially since we lived so far away from them throughout our childhood. Many times my mother would explain how she had always wanted a sister closer in age so she could share her girly secrets and clothes growing up. Both of her sisters lived with us at one point in their lives. My father always expressed his devotion to his family by welcoming his siblings to live with us and taking the burden from his parents. We always had a designated time to share a meal and weekends were for the family. That's just how we were raised.

Till this day, I turn off the ringer on my cell phone during meals and confide in my mother and sisters for advice on everything. They do the same. When we all get together for holidays we find our roles as children back in place. Suzanne smelling her food, Nini being told to eat more, and I serve the food with *Mami*. Although *Papi* is not around, we acknowledge his presence through a memory or by confessing our childhood mischief to our mother for the ten millionth time or even our adult mischief for the first time. On one particular Thanksgiving, we decided to tell *Mami* about the time we did a group bungee jump several years earlier. At the time of the jump, we were all over eighteen. The three of us were harnessed together into

Las Niñas

a giant slingshot that overlooked a bar in South Padre Island. Our *Tío* Paco, *Papi's* younger brother, paid for us to be flung through 150 feet of air. Our mother was not very amused even though we all agreed that *Papi* would have been. It's funny how even now as adults we find ourselves debating whether to share a particular story with our mother.

There have also been times where I noticed that *Papi* was not mentioned at all during our special gathering. Those moments reassured me that he was with us. After all, we still find time to spend moments together as we were taught. That's probably one of the best accomplishments that *Papi* and *Mami* achieved as parents.

Chapter Three

Ch-air, ch-air, chair!

Ironically, now while teaching primary English in Beijing, China, I am reminded of my own childhood nightmares in Elementary school. It is not apparent today, but Spanish was my first language. For the first four years of my life I lived near my grandparents who only spoke Spanish, and were surrounded by a Spanish-speaking environment in Brownsville, Texas.

I didn't study English intensively until I started school in Southern California. My mother reminds me often, as well as many other people occasionally, that as a young child I used to speak Spanish perfectly. I think the constant reminders while growing up, made me realize that my Spanish was not so perfect, which would explain why I always insisted on studying it throughout my school years. I even minored in Spanish during college. I am definitely not complaining about my experience. Being bilingual opened many doors for me in the workplace before I had a degree. I have to admit, I am quite empathetic to anyone who has to learn English as a second language and still find a way to keep his or her family's native language.

I still remember vividly the times throughout my childhood in which I was repeatedly corrected in class for pronouncing a word incorrectly or with an accent. In the late nineteen seventies and early eighties there was no such thing as bilingual classes for children at schools, which in the long run, had advantages as well as disadvantages. Not only were teachers forced to mainstream—children who had trouble with English pronunciation in with the "regular" students, but their training didn't address this new dilemma within our society. To make matters more difficult, they did have an ESL (English as a Second Language) class for bilingual students, however it usually meant you were taken out of the regular class session to improve your English. It caused a greater disadvantage than being singled out in class, and ran the risk of a student falling behind in their studies and possibly not passing to the next grade.

I asked my sister Suzanne for her opinion on this topic. She has taught bilingual classes and recently obtained her Masters of Arts in Elementary Education. She confirmed that ESL classes are still conducted in a similar manner in some school systems to this day. Unfortunately, leading statistics prove that ESL courses are the least successful in helping students "perform" on standardized exams. Within the most recent years, Suzanne's opinion has progressed from seeing the various bilingual teaching methods as a form of segregation in the school system, to actively promoting the curriculum's full potential to succeed.

During my first years in school, I was asked by the new teachers if English or Spanish was my first language. At the time, I didn't know the reason behind the question. I proudly answered "Spanish!" That same day I was sent to ESL class and a note was sent home to my parents. The next morning my parents accompanied me to school and there was some kind of confrontation in which the teacher appeared angry and was told that I would no longer attend ESL classes. This apparently happened to many bilingual students. Eventually my parents coached me to state that English was my first language. My parents were very creative when explaining to me that it was okay to lie to my teacher for that particular reason.

For my first five years of elementary school I was trying to lose my Spanish and the accent that lingered when I spoke English. I began to lose my Mexican pride, since the teachers focused on it so much, and started assimilating with the American culture. At the time I was only a child who expressed this by feeling resentment and embarrassment. Unfortunately, the repercussions only got worse. We all began to speak English at home, which started to concern my parents and embarrass them when we would correct their English. A firm rule was set that we could not speak English at home, simply so we could practice our Spanish and hold on to our family's culture.

My parents were unaware of the constant turmoil I faced at school by not practicing my English at home. There were two different occasions in fourth grade in which I actually started to cry in class due to the learning method my teacher decided to implement. On the first occasion, I was asked to read the word "chair" out loud. I said what sounded like "share." I was then asked to stand up and repeat the word while facing the class. I repeatedly said it incorrectly. The teacher insisted that I could not return to my seat until the word was pronounced accurately. After numerous attempts, I could feel my eyes fill with tears and there was an immense pressure in my chest. I started twiddling my fingers and stared at the ceiling instead of my classmates, who only expressed blank looks on their faces after my many attempts to say the word "ch-air." I got so frustrated with myself because each attempt sounded perfect in my head, but the sound never seemed to make it through my mouth. It was as if it got stuck somewhere between my Mexican pride and the voice of my blonde teacher insisting that I needed to try again.

At some point, the pressure in my chest manifested to a hysterical cry that switched my focus

Las Niñas

from saying, "ch-air" to just being able to breathe. The teacher seemed a bit remorseful and asked me quite nicely to return to my seat. She tried to continue with her lesson, but all arms ceased from being raised, especially by the Spanish-speaking students. No one, not even the white students, tried to be the teacher's pet at that moment. The lesson was quickly changed to another subject.

The next pronunciation incident occurred during the week when it was our class' turn to put on a performance in front of the whole school. Of course, each student was expected to participate by speaking into a microphone in front the entire campus. Before my part was even assigned to me, I was already loathing the idea. Surely the teacher wasn't going to choose me. She couldn't, not with the accent I had. Apparently, she believed in the "equal opportunity" policy the school district implemented because, sure enough, I was chosen as the host speaker. I never understood why she insisted on making me speak. It was bad enough that I hated just speaking English since the whole "ch-air" incident, but now this same teacher wanted to further embarrass me by forcing me to speak to the entire student body. Not only was I supposed to introduce our class, but I had to start out the presentation with "A is for..."

This time, the teacher decided to have her class assistant take over the rest of the lesson while she helped me practice the speech just outside the classroom door. I still managed to get frustrated and cry, but this time the teacher said "Good job, just try your best and it will be all right, ok?" I sniffled and said "Ok."

A couple of days later I was standing in front of the entire school. *Mami* had done my hair with a big red bow. I was wearing my Sunday clothes, but still felt very ugly and nervous. There were hundreds, maybe not hundreds, but at that age, thirty people felt like a hundred, of students and teachers staring at me. I took a deep breath and asked God to help me. I said a prayer in my head so I could talk to him in Spanish. "Okay here it goes. Just try your best." my teacher said. The microphone was turned on so my deep breaths echoed out to the crowd. Teachers began to smile and students were waiting for me to say something. As the words came out, I could hear them, not just in my head, but flowing perfectly towards the crowd, "A IS for..."

When it was time for me to walk away, I looked over to my teacher and I remember her winking at me. I knew I had done my best. Whether her teaching techniques were appropriate or not, she was just doing her best, too. This was a new era in time for all of us, things were changing, people were changing, and it was apparent different languages were surfacing into the school system. Just like my parents had to find a way for me to receive a fair education and still manage to keep my first language, my teacher and I had to find a way to learn from each other and try our best. Together we all did just that – tried our best. Since then, all words in English or Spanish began to feel more natural. I can't remember what "A" is for because all I can recall is how to say, "A" and "is" separately. I obviously had trouble with my speech. It was too difficult for me to separate out "A" and "is." I would pronounce it as "A's." I think it was due to nervousness, and until this day, I still speak too fast, but my confidence has most definitely improved. Now I'm told I speak too much in both English and Spanish. *Muchas gracias*[3], to my fourth grade teacher!

[3] *Thank you very much*

Las Niñas

Now throughout America, numerous school districts have incorporated bilingual classes into the elementary schools. While writing this story, Suzanne continued to assist me and indulge me with her own recent experiences on this topic. Bilingual classes are not just part of our recent generations. This method was implemented in the states when the first immigrants arrived, namely the Germans and the French. In addition, Texas used the same method for dealing with the students from Mexico.

My parents both were sent to bilingual classes when they arrived in Texas in the late nineteen sixties. I realize now that my parents were protecting us by not letting us be placed in ESL classes so that we wouldn't experience what they had. The impact this system had on the both of them was completely different. My father, in time, learned to accept the change and practiced on a daily basis to improve his English and accent. I recall as a child, sitting around the dinner table practicing difficult words with him, especially when it came time for his reviews at work and interviews for a promotion. I can proudly say that he started in the pressroom as a janitor and ten years later, a month before he passed away, he not only received a head supervisor position in the print room, but was also inaugurated as a U.S. citizen.

My mother, on the other hand, reprimanded us when we corrected her English as children. She felt we were being disrespectful and reminded us that we also spoke Spanish. Once we got older and still witnessed my mother making common mistakes such as pronouncing a neighbor's name as "Bicki" instead of "Vicki" or, an embarrassing moment for Nini and her eleven year old classmates, when she suggested eating at "Fuckruckers" instead of "Fudruckers," we had to ask why she didn't make the effort to improve her English, especially since we lived in a predominantly "white" neighborhood. She shared her experience learning English as a second language with us and we never questioned it again.

She was susceptible to ridicule from her peers, including Mexican students that felt they were superior to her simply because they understood more English than she did. Her innate reaction was to reject the English language and hold on to her accent. She says her accent represents who she is and how she got to America. To this day, she has avoided obtaining her citizenship. She continues to fight against assimilation and acquiring her American accent. During one discussion in her new home in Miami, my mother managed to impress me and enlighten my viewpoints on assimilation, but only after I criticized her by saying her accent had gotten worse since she moved to Miami. She responded, saying, "What do you mean I have an accent? *¿Y qué importa? El minuto que caminas afuera encuentras "Americanos" que tienen acentos de todas partes del mundo! A todos se les olvida que sus padres también tenían acento cuando llegaron.* Maybe they need to assimilate to OUR America, not me to theirs."[4]

My mother will probably never admit to this, but her lack of English led to her lack of education. The teaching methods combined with the ridicule instilled in her a feeling of insecurity in this new country, only led her to regret not having obtained a higher education.

---

[4] What do you mean I have an accent? Why does it matter? The minute you walk outside you find "Americans" that have accents from all over the world! Everyone seems to forget that their parents also had accents when they arrived. Maybe they need to assimilate to OUR America, not me to theirs.

Las Niñas

I have to admit that I, as well as my sisters, sometimes think less of her and don't seek her opinion on some subjects due to her lack of education. I find that many people associate an accent or lack of English with the person not being knowledgeable or in many cases incapable. There are moments like the conversation that I mentioned that remind us of *Mami*'s life experiences and her intellect, and now we proudly encourage her to return to school. Unfortunately, she still undermines herself by using her age as an excuse.

As I mentioned before, English as a second language in any school system has both its advantages and disadvantages. We continue to strive to assimilate into this new American culture. When I say "we," it's no longer just us Mexicans. "We" is everyone in America, first, second, third and all generations. Mexicans, Chinese, Irish, German, Colombians, Afghanis, Persians, Jewish, Venezuelans, Vietnamese, and Japanese, are all American.

This assimilation is being felt by everyone involved. It's in our school system, government, military, the local bar, and shopping mall. Each day we encounter a new shift, a new problem, and a new success story. Each day a child feels resentment and embarrassment while a parent contemplates if they have made the right choice for their child. Each day I am proud to say I am Mexican-American. As times change, so do the people of our country, and so will the daily struggles and success stories that our teachers embrace.

Chapter Four

Nuestra Mami

As an adult, I have really grown to appreciate my mother. I can't really say she has always been who she is now, a confident, salsa dancing, margarita drinking, beautiful, almost fifty-four year-old mother. I think each person becomes who he or she needs to be for that particular moment in time. During our childhood, my mother was who she needed to be for us. She was the traditional *Madre Mexicana*[5].

Nuestra mami[6] had many nicknames that we heard growing up. First, she was *Mami* of course, but then we discovered she was Sara, *China*, *Gorda*, and *Vieja*[7], but with us she eventually became mom.

My mother was named after her grandmother. She was the second child, but first girl of seven children. She grew up mostly with her brothers who were the children of my grandmother's first marriage. My uncles gave my mother the Spanish nickname "China," because she had long straight hair and almond shaped eyes.

Our mother stayed home to raise us through most of our childhood. She maintained the house and cooked for us every day. Our mother stayed home to raise us through most of our childhood. She maintained the house and cooked for us every day.

[5] *Mexican mother.*

[6] *Our mother.*

[7] *Chinese girl, fat lady and old lady.*

Las Niñas

She made traditional Mexican food and her rice was her trademark. To this day, we've never been able to compete with her Mexican rice. Our mother did everything from preparing our meals to hand making our prize winning Halloween costumes. She was the perfect host and a devoted Catholic mother. She catered to her husband, children, and church. She did all of this starting at the age of seventeen and had her three children by the age of twenty-two, before she could even acknowledge how much of a woman she really was.

The first time I realized my mother was an attractive woman was when she was in her mid to late twenties. We were at Knott's Berry Farm, an amusement park in Southern California. We sat pretty close to the front stage to watch a live entertainment show. The host was performing random acts, which included singing popular songs. At one point, he was singing a love song and came off the stage to take my mother's hand. I looked at my father and he was grinning at the sight. I, on the other hand, instantly became jealous for my father and embarrassed for my mother. I shifted from my seat and started to get very angry. Tears formed in my eyes and my dad reassured me it was ok. As the song proceeded, I stared at my mother and the rude man.

Several lines into the song, I thought to myself how could he not pick out my mother? I looked around and realized she was probably the prettiest woman there. I never really noticed how beautiful my mother was until that day. She was wearing khaki short shorts and a Hawaiian print loose top. Her hair was chestnut brown, long, and wavy at the ends. She had clear, fair skin and didn't wear much make-up. Her shorts showed off her long, slender legs while her modesty amplified her natural beauty. Everyone in the crowd was staring at her with a smile. That's when I realized they too thought she was pretty. By the end of the song, my mother's face had changed from her usual rosy color to a bright red, and she truly seemed to be embarrassed. I was still a little upset by the scene, but she was too consumed in her moment to even notice, which I am very glad she didn't. As the clapping and whistling poured out at the end of the song, I think she also realized for the first time that not only did my father appreciate her simple beauty, but so did everyone else.

I think it's difficult for children to acknowledge their parents are just as human as they are. I have to say the opposite is also true, parents place their children on these pedestals that often seem impossible to reach. Both parties are astonished when their priceless object suddenly becomes popular or even just ordinary. Until that day at the amusement park, my mother was not a sexy woman, she was just mi *Mami* and *Papi's Gorda*.[8] I often have said I just want to meet a man that would stare at me as my father stared at my mother that day.

Growing up, it has been hard to admit that my mother was not an educated woman, at times just a housewife, possibly a potential divorcee, and truly a guilt stricken widow. What I have come to realize is that my mother can be anything she wants to be, good or bad, and nobody has the right to judge her actions just because she is our mother.

Mami is just as beautiful, unique, and fragile as the rest of us. She had to sacrifice the first forty years of her life and at times endure the greatest criticism of all from her family and herself.

[8] *My mommy and Daddy's fat wife (meaning transpires to a husband or son referring to their wife or mother as their "old lady")*

Las Niñas

    She has done something quite remarkable that has made those who once criticized her actions voice out loud their sincere compliments. She has raised three independent women that have been able to embrace their culture as well as their own lives. Now, my mother spends her days under the sun and on the beaches of Miami, free from her past and finally living her own life. She is no longer trapped into her role as a daughter, sister, wife, mother, sister-in-law, or the perfect image we created in our heads for her to be. She is just another person doing a little soul searching and getting to know herself, Sara Elba Bustamante.

Chapter Five

¡Patas de Rana! Frog legs?

Our parents always found a way to bring different cultures into our home. Many times they would invite *Papi's* coworkers or church friends to our family barbeques and birthday celebrations. As an adult, I appreciate these introductions to diversity, especially when it exposed me to a variety of food. *Papi* worked in the printing area of the Orange County Register, and most of his coworkers were other immigrants with backgrounds similar to his. All were new to America from various countries such as the Philippines, Vietnam, Pacific Islands, Colombia, and many different regions in Mexico. On occasion he would exchange his lunch with a friend at work and insisted on saving it for his girls at home, simply so we could taste a different type of food. It was never enough food for a meal but it was definitely plenty to provide an evening of amusement for *las niñas*! He would not only make us taste this weird food, but would also share a story about his friend and where he came from. Sometimes the stories included hardships that his friends had encountered, and would explain how we would one day be able to visit that country too.

One particular evening, my father came home with a handful of groceries. *Papi* would often cook dinner during our childhood. There were several periods when *Mami* insisted on working, which meant she and *Papi* shared the household responsibilities. We were going to be introduced to some rare food. I'm not sure how he came up with this idea or if he had read about it in the food section of that day's paper, but *Papi* was eager to cook frog legs for us. The four of us sat around the table asking *Papi* all kinds of questions about dinner. He consistently responded "*¡Es una sorpresa! ¡No se pueden acercar a la cocina!* It's a surprise! You are not allowed near the kitchen!" We would laugh and tease him about dinner from a distance. I recall yelling out, "Is it *tacos*? Is it hot dogs?"

"I hope its chocolate cake!" Suzanne yelled. Whatever it was, we heard it sizzling in the kitchen and it smelled different. When mom ran over to make sure he was not burning our dinner, he pushed her away in a joking manner and said, "When have I ever burned our food?"

"*Nunca sabes*...You never know..." she replied.

It finally came to the time when he brought dinner to the table, and by then we had set the table as usual with plates, silverware, and drinks for five. *Papi* walked in carrying a plate over his head so we couldn't see it until it was placed on the table. All we had in front of us was a bottle of ketchup, and it appeared that it was also our only side dish. As he set the plate down, we all stretched our necks with curiosity. There was a mound of what looked like skinny legs.

"¡*Ay* Rafa! How do you eat this?" my mother screamed.

"Just try it. It tastes like chicken," *Papi* said.

"What is it?" Nini asked.

"¡*Patas de Rana*!" he said very proudly.

"Frog legs?" we all stated with disgust.

My mother immediately refused as he placed a couple of them on each of our plates. I added ketchup on the side and started imitating what *Papi* was doing.

Nini followed the same process, and we cut them up in small pieces, dipped them in ketchup, and forced pieces into our mouths. With big smiles of relief, we agreed that it tasted like chicken. *Mami* cleared her plate and went to find something else to eat. We all looked at Suzanne and reminded her that it tasted like chicken but she still hesitated. She was shocked to see us actually eating our frog legs. "But it reminds me of Kermit the frog!" Suzanne stated.

I guess it never occurred to *Papi* that our childhood friend was being served for dinner. He tried to make a game out of it so Suzanne would join us in this new experience that he later explained was part of French culture. He pretended she was a baby by playing "airplane" with a piece of frog leg on a fork. She placed her hand over her mouth and shouted, "I am not eating Kermit!" *Papi* then suggested that Nini and I should hold her down while he placed it in her mouth, and we rushed eagerly to her side. She quickly squirmed out of her seat, crawled under the table, and sprinted out of the dining area.

"¡Córrele mija! Run daughter!" shouted our mother. We all chased after her, laughing out loud. *Papi* stabbed an entire leg with his fork and followed his girls into the chase. Nini and I saw *Papi* and ran back for frog legs of our own to chase her with. Suzanne ran around the living room, climbing over the furniture and running around the coffee table. *Papi* swept her up and placed her on the floor while we tried to hold her arms and tickle her to open her mouth.

"No!" she screamed while mom watched from a distance with amusement. We all waved frog legs in front of her face teasing her with "Eat Kermit or else!" threats. We never really meant to put any in her mouth, but out of nowhere, *Papi* tore a piece off and placed it in her mouth. Suzanne was completely shocked, but she knew better than to spit it out. She chewed a piece and said, "It does taste like chicken!" We all started laughing and ate the frog legs we had in our hands. By the end of the evening even *Mami* joined us in finishing up the mound of frog legs. Kermit didn't taste so bad after all.

Growing up, I realized my parents were not as typical as I made them out to be. They tried their hardest to raise us as a typical Mexican family, but in all honesty, they weren't typical themselves. One lesson that my parents repeatedly introduced to us was diversity. If we ever stated that we were "Mexican," my parents would correct us by stating "Mexican-American." They reinforced our pride for both cultures even though they have countless stories about the prejudice they faced in their new country. They made every attempt possible to expose us to different cultures and people. They expressed the importance of equality and being assertive in life. In a way, *Papi's* introductions to different types of food initiated the acceptance within us.

The diversity among the kids in the neighborhood reinforced the things my parents taught us. Some of my childhood playmates consisted of African-Americans, Tongans, Samoans, Chinese-Americans, Mexicans, and Caucasian Americans. We learned at a young age that everyone was the same and there was no need to fear the unknown or unfamiliar. *Papi* and *Mami* even befriended the two men that shared a home together at the end of the block. Our neighbors became our adopted grandparents even though they were white. *Papi* often shared a beer with the Tongans and Samoans even when their islands had a long history of rivalry. Once I got older my mother repeatedly told me "I don't care who you date. He can be black, brown, white or even green. All that matters is that he treats you good."

Needless to say it might have been the "*patas de rana*" that helped us to define the diversity in our lives. Without such experiences I think we may have passed up the opportunity to accept and love new cultures and people.

Chapter Six

Abuela Cata y Las Primas

One of the many advantages of growing up in the first generation of our family born in America is the bond we are able to maintain with our cousins. *Las primas*[9] consisted of Cathy, Angie, Vanessa, and the three of us. Carmelita, now Carmen, is my grandmother's youngest child, she happens to be the same age as my youngest sister and was also born in America. My mother and *Abuela* Cata[10] shared an interesting bond that many mothers and daughters don't get to share. They were both pregnant with their last children at the same time. My "aunt" Carmen was born five months before Nini, so she is about three years younger than I am. We have always treated her like one of our cousins rather than an aunt.

The seven of us grew up together over the summers. Since we lived in California and Cathy traveled with her parents through the Air Force, all of our parents made an effort to get together over the summers, either in Texas with our *Abuela Cata* and the rest of the cousins, or through a family reunion in Southern California.

Even now that we are all adults, we still find ourselves gathered occasionally around our grandmothers' table playfully disputing who is grandma's favorite. Since our younger days, our family has expanded quite a bit.

[9] *The Cousins.*

[10] *Grandmother Cata; Cata is a nickname derived from her full name Catalina.*

Younger cousins are currently in their late teens and early twenties. Angie and Carmen have children of their own, making it quite difficult to compete with the younger members of the family for grandma's attention.

Our parents allowed us to visit grandma because they expected her to be an ideal babysitter. To tell you the truth, *Abuela* Cata was far from being the traditional *Mexicana* grandmother model. The only tradition she maintained religiously was trying to feed us *frijoles*[11] and homemade flour *tortillas*. She was very young and active for a grandmother.

Staying with *Abuela* meant freedom from the restrictions on junk food, set bedtimes, and household rules. The majority of the time, we ran around without any supervision. On occasion, Angie's and Vanessa's parents would take a day off to shuttle us around to the public pool or nearby movie theatres. We would mostly walk around Dallas visiting my Aunt Juana to get free food at the fast food place she worked at.

That summer in Dallas, our grandmother was employed at an onion warehouse. She left early in the morning and would return late in the afternoon. Sometimes our *Tío* Ramón or Tía Juana[12] were around for some mediocre supervision that included us always pestering them until they eventually left with the money grandma left for us. They always promised us junk food, but never came back at a reasonable time. On one occasion, Ramón took over three hours to pick up lunch, which consisted of two pizzas, one for him and one for the rest of us to share.

---

[11] *Beans*

[12] *Uncle Ramón or Aunt Juana.*

Las Niñas

Once, *Tío* Ramón stormed out of the cramped apartment. Since he left, we all agreed to go swimming without permission. Almost all of us could swim pretty good and those who didn't, knew to stay in the shallow end or use the floats to stay above water. I was eleven years old. Suzanne, Cathy and Angie were nine, and Nini, Vanessa, and Carmelita were all around seven.

As we paraded around the apartment changing into our swimsuits and preparing our snacks for the pool, I rambled off the rules to the girls.

"Nini, Vanessa, and Carmelita, you can't go into the deep end, even if you have a floaty, okay? No one can tell our parents or *Abuela* that we went or we will all get in trouble! If Ramón comes home, he won't tell if we agree not to tell grandma he took the money, so remember that OK?"

"Yeah we know, Sarah! OK!" they all responded.

We marched out of the apartment with towels wrapped around our waists and bags filled with chips, sandwiches, cokes, and cookies. Walking down the stairs, we noticed that the Texas weather had changed as it often did. The sun was not blazing above us but somehow the heat wave still hovered over the black turf in the parking lot. The gray clouds were moving closer to the apartment, but we ignored their presence and never mentioned the weather.

As we approached the swimming pool, small raindrops began to land on our faces. Simultaneously, all of us began to laugh and sing.

"It's raining, it's pouring, the old man is snoring. It's raining, it's pouring, RAMÓN is always snoring. He bumped his head getting out of bed, and he couldn't wake up in the morning!" The laughter of young girls filled the area of the swimming pool. We continued to ignore the rain and jumped into the pool for our splash fight. Moments after we jumped in, we heard the loud noise that made all of us acknowledge the presence of the Texas storm that came to ruin our picnic at the pool. Thunder could be heard and lightening had become visible at a distance.

We all knew that we shouldn't have been in the pool to begin with, and the lightning only made it more apparent. I instructed all the girls to get out of the pool. They didn't listen, and I only got them to wait on the side of the pool with their feet dangling in the water. We spent the next hour sitting by the pool, eating soggy sandwiches and picking *piojos* out of each other's hair. Unfortunately, the storm never let up. We packed our stuff and headed back to the apartment so we could get home before grandma.

Walking up the stairs, we noticed grandma starting her usual routine of undressing with an old sheet barely draped around her. Since she works at the onion warehouse, she avoids bringing her clothes into the apartment because they stink up the cozy home. Seeing us out of the corner of her eye, she re-adjusted the falling sheet and yelled, "¡Ay niñas! ¡No me digan que estaban en la piscina! Ay Girls! Don't tell me you were at the pool!" The other girls all looked at me.

"No *Abuela*, we just walked over there, but it started raining so we came back." I replied. She mumbled that she didn't believe us, but it didn't matter. The seven of us sheepishly followed our half naked *Abuela* into the apartment.

Abuela immediately started to prepare dinner as we placed ourselves in front of the TV. All of sudden, we heard the radio turn on in the kitchen and heard the sound of a beer popping open. We enjoy watching our grandmother prepare dinner because it's filled with dancing and singing. Suzanne stood up to go to

Las Niñas

the restroom, but didn't make it past the kitchen. As soon as *Abuela* caught sight of Suzanne, she became her next dance partner.

In the midst of her giggles, Suzanne started squealing "*Abuela!*" We rushed over to watch the live entertainment. *Abuela* and Suzanne were dancing in the small kitchen to a *ranchera* (traditional Mexican country music) while food sizzled on the stove and the aroma of hot peppers tickled our throats. The same cries of laughter that flooded the pool, transcend among the natural sounds of a spicy Mexican kitchen, and Suzanne squirms off to the restroom. The younger girls take turns trying to run past the kitchen, but seem to find a way into grandma's arms.

After dinner, we sat around the living room watching *Abuela*'s *novelas*[13] while she sprayed Raid on the younger girls' hair to kill the *piojos*[14]. No one really questioned anything grandma did, we just thought that it was the way she did things. As the evening came closer, we initiated our daily survey of whose turn it might have been to sleep with grandma. She always insists that one of us sleep with her since she missed us being near her. Carmelita was always exempt from this chore because she lived with our grandmother and slept with her on a daily basis.

The issue wasn't that we didn't want to sleep with her, but that we had to fall asleep before her to tune out the loud snoring that kept us awake all night. *Abuela* snored very loud and most of the time we couldn't sleep.

[13] *Mexican soap operas.*

[14] *Lice*

We would often sneak out of her room. Carmelita tried to give us tips like shoving her or telling her to be quiet, but none of us ever dared to do that because, after all, she was our grandmother. Whoever ended up sleeping with her had to also sacrifice the late movies and snacks that often lasted to all hours of the night. Once the matter was settled, one of us would go to sleep on grandma's bed, and the rest would fall asleep sporadically in the living room.

Looking back at our childhood memories, I have learned to appreciate the closeness our culture extends to our entire family. Even though we were multiple states away, we made an effort to communicate with *Abuela* and *las primas*, either by phone or through annual visits. Nowadays, *Abuela* spends less time making tortillas and more time raising the next generation. She still plays her *rancheras* and upon a special visit or occasion, she'll make any favorite dish upon request.

Mmm...I can still taste her *sopes con carne molida*[15] while I overhear high-pitched laughter and requests from *mis primas* for the next *tortilla de harina*.[16]

---

[15] *Ground beef.*

[16] *Flour tortilla.*

Chapter Seven

Sacramento or Bust!

One of the last family vacations we had with *Papi* was our road trip through California. I bet it was *Papi's* idea because I can't imagine *Mami* eagerly seeking to be trapped in an old beat up camper for two weeks with six girls ranging from the age of eight through twelve.

This is our most memorable summer reunion with our cousins. Unfortunately, Cathy was in Germany with her family, so she was unable to attend. Angie, Vanessa, and Carmen flew in from Dallas for one month. We started our road trip from our home in Santa Ana, and it required at least three days of preparation and tedious trips to the grocery store.

Mami and *Papi* were very good at being frugal. They insisted in bringing along everything we would possibly need to avoid making any unnecessary purchases along the way. I'm not sure it worked, but it was a family ritual. It took us about two hours to get out of the driveway, but once we did, there was no stopping us.

The camper looked run down, and we made sure to tell *Papi* what we thought. We even asked if we could get another one. I am sure it dented his *machismo* pride a little, as it would have done to any proud Mexican father, but as children we were unaware of the many overnight shifts he muddled throughout to earn this vacation. The camper housed a small living area, a kitchen with a table, a restroom with a shower, and a sleeping area by the driver's seat.

The table turned into a bed, and my parents claimed it as their sleeping quarters. Four of us girls slept in the overhead area, and the other two slept on the benches in the so-called living room. It was a tight fit, but it made the trip even more interesting.

At the time, I was a depressed pre-teen. I was not a little girl anymore, but wasn't confident enough to do anything on my own. The trip was a horrible idea in my eyes, but in retrospect, it was the last summer I spent as a child. I plan to take the trip again one day, but it will be with my own family.

Our first stop was a very beautiful beach near San Luis Obispo. We spent the night in the parking lot and encountered our first incident that night. Carmen rolled off the overhead bed and landed on the floor. Unfortunately, the whole family woke up to her crying, but luckily, the only thing she suffered from was a major scare in the middle of the night. After that, my parents padded the floor with extra pillows and blankets to prevent anyone else from falling out of the overhead compartment. Needless to say, Carmen never slept up there again even though no one else managed to fall off. Waking up on the beach was a big treat for all of us, and to this day, I couldn't have imagined a better way to wake up.

Our trip consisted of visiting several beaches and making significant stops in Lake Tahoe, Sequoia and Yosemite National Parks, San Francisco, and in the state capitol, Sacramento. The next episode in our trip occurred after my mother realized the small refrigerator was not working very well. The outlet was slightly loose, and the refrigerator had spent some time unplugged, causing some of the contents to soften and melt. The items mostly affected were prime ingredients for our favorite meal, peanut butter and jelly.

That afternoon, we all ordered peanut butter and jelly sandwiches from my mother. Not long after, we all began to have stomach issues. First, it was just my sister Suzanne, who rudely stated out loud that she had diarrhea. She proceeded to describe it.

"It's like I was peeing from my butt!" she said. We began to laugh and make fun of her. My mother told us that we needed to tell her if we were sick too. Soon after, we all started making trips to the restroom. It got to a point where we had to take turns to avoid an embarrassing moment. My parents made a pit stop at a drugstore and stocked up on Pepto Bismo, but it didn't help fast enough. Angie squirmed while waiting for Carmen to get out of the incredibly stinking bathroom. Everyone cringed every time the door opened.

"Hurry Carmen, I really have to go!" Angie cried.

"I'm trying Angie! I can't help it!" Carmen shouted back. She soon rushed out from the bathroom, buttoning her pants. Angie ran in, but started to cry in the process. She didn't make it, and tried frantically to sit on the toilet.

During all of this, my father was driving to our next destination, probably using it as an excuse to escape the nightmare my mother had to deal with. While Angie was attempting to sit on the toilet, my father made a sharp right turn, sending Angie off the toilet and onto the floor with her soiled pants down. My mother rushed to her rescue, as we all covered our faces in an attempt to minimize Angie's embarrassment. My mother commanded my father to stop at a public restroom so she could clean and sanitize our temporary living arrangements.

That evening, we were heading north on Pacific Coast Highway when our camper began making a weird noise and hesitated to go any faster. Cars started to honk at us as they passed by. My father pulled over to the side of the road and told us that we would have to spend the evening on the freeway. Our mother was very concerned, but there wasn't much they could do since there was no way of calling for help. None of us could sleep because big trucks would drive by and make our camper sway side to side. We passed the time talking and giggling, while my parents shared whispers of their own.

In the middle of the night, we heard a knock at the door. My parents jumped up and my mother whispered for us to be quiet. My father was weary of what might be outside, and grabbed the broom for defense. He peeked out the window, and told mom he was going to answer the door. A rather scary, old man greeted him. He had a long white beard, scruffy clothing, and a big beer belly that hung over his jeans. He reminded me of one of the guys on the cover of the ZZ Top albums that my uncle Ramón listened to.

My father and the old man exchanged words, leading to our exit from the camper. The man stated that it wasn't safe for us to sit on the side of the road, especially with children aboard. He insisted on helping us get to a safer place, and followed our dying camper to the nearest gas station two exits away. Once we arrived, he called a friend for help.

We stood outside while mosquitoes fed off our arms and legs. Suzanne and Angie started to complain first. Carmelita slapped Angie on the arm.

"Ah, look I got one, Angie!" she said. We all began to smack each other. *Mami* ran inside the camper, grabbed the insect repellent, and began spraying all of us. I suggested that she spray Papi, but he waved her away.

Las Niñas

"*Los mosquitos no me pican a mí, mi sangre está muy agria, solo les gustan la sangre dulce como la de ustedes.* The mosquitoes don't bite me, my blood is too sour; they only like sweet blood like yours," he said with a smile. Our camper was towed and the men dropped us off at a modest motel nearby. *Mami* expressed her opinion against the idea, but *Papi* trusted the men to come back for him the next morning.

We were supposed to be on the road again the next afternoon, but due to the unexpected expenses on the camper and motel, our trip changed. It's always been difficult for my father to tell us he can't afford to do something he really wants to do. It was apparent that he felt ashamed. We told him that we didn't care and that we liked being in the camper, but Lake Tahoe was taken off our list of places to visit.

Sequoia Park was the next stop after the camper was fixed. The trees towered around us as if we were fairies in some fantasy world. The view was astonishing. The bark on the trees was a deep red color and we got to drive through one of the tree trunks. We took plenty of pictures and amused ourselves by pretending we were Tinkerbell from Peter Pan.

That evening we arrived at Yosemite Park, which was also an incredible site. Greenery and mountains surround us on every side. We were relieved to see other campers filled with families. We got there early enough to prepare *carne asada*, but had to wait until the next morning to begin our exploration.

Yosemite was a completely different experience for all of us. We were surrounded by wilderness. A stream was located right behind our camper, mountains and waterfalls were seen at a distance, and numerous hiking trails could be found within twenty feet of our camping site. The next morning, we all jumped out of bed and rushed outside. *Papi* joined us while *Mami* slept in and recuperated from the previous days. My favorite scene at Yosemite was a tree we encountered on one of the hiking trails. As we walked through miles of grass and enormous trees, *Papi* pointed out a tree that had fallen to the ground a long time ago. It served as the perfect photo landmark. I noticed a crevice in the middle of it, as I leaned over to peer into it. I felt the other girls pushing their way towards the tree as well.

"Papi, thousands of ladybugs are in here!" I shouted. It was incredible to see so many of them. *Papi* insisted we leave them alone and avoid disturbing them. We are all too curious to do so. I had to touch one of them. As I placed my hand on the tree, the red and black creatures quickly decorated it. They tickled my hand and I couldn't control my laughter. *Papi's* camera clicked and he decided it was best to leave with that memory. He carefully pushed the ladybugs from my hand, and we made our way to the next trail.

Not too long after we started on the next trail, my father took a potty break and walked off into the bushes. Angie had missed his comment and continued to follow him as if it was part of the trail. Angie came running back towards us doubled over in laughter while *Papi* yelled at us to stay where we were. I guess you can't expect too much privacy when surrounded by six lively girls.

Papi enjoyed every minute of our trip. At times he stopped to talk to some of the neighbors, who always ask if all of us are his daughters. He proudly nodded yes and always stated that he wouldn't have it any other way. People never seemed to doubt him, I think because being Mexican often means you come from a big family. *Papi* was used to being surrounded by women, especially since he grew up with five younger siblings, four of whom were girls.

Our climb up the waterfalls, ended up with me slipping and falling into a big puddle of water. *Mami* insisted that we stop climbing and come down for our own safety. *Papi* on the other hand, saw it as a once in a lifetime opportunity and continued up the side of the waterfall against mother's wishes. We watched him climb high up and then saw him turn and wave.

That's one of the best memories I have of my father, always trying to live life to the fullest. He died about a year and half later, and I wonder if he knew then that he would never climb a waterfall again.

We stayed in Yosemite for several days, one of which was a long day of rainfall that took us by surprise while on a paddleboat. The water level rose quickly, making it difficult to maneuver. We lost control and were headed straight towards the waterfall. The only guard placed for safety was a yellow rope attached to a sign that read "Danger – Keep Away." We tried to do just that and were peddling as fast as we could. Somehow we survived. Upon arriving at our campsite, we discovered that our items left by the fire pit were floating down the stream. My mom was trying to fish them out herself but couldn't save everything fast enough. *Papi* jumped into the stream and threw the items towards us. We were all laughing uncontrollably. The whole vacation had been such an ordeal, so that incident was no surprise. We ended the day by packing and playing Scrabble in the camper. The next day we said goodbye to our neighbors and headed out to San Francisco.

The rest of the trip and the ride home were a bit of a blur. I think our enthusiasm was left behind in Yosemite. Once we arrived in San Francisco, our parents rented a big station wagon capable of hauling all of us around town. The station wagon matched our camper's characteristics. I don't know where my father found those rental companies, but by the looks of our monsters of transportation, it was obviously based on price and convenience. I'm sure it was quite the site for those who happened to witness our eight-foot station wagon slowly taking the curves on Lombardi Street. We didn't spend much time in San Francisco but did visit a park where my parents got sucked into a timeshare presentation. I think they stayed for the free gift. I don't know what gift they received, but we didn't join the timeshare. Sacramento was equally uneventful, although it was our main topic of conversation when we returned to school that fall, simply because we could say we visited the capitol of California.

Although a trip on the Pacific Coast Highway doesn't seem like the type of adventure that would lead someone to participate in building latrines in Honduras for three months, parade through Mexico or Italy with a suitcase, or even move to China to teach English, it was just that. These memories contributed to our travels as adults. All three of us have ventured across borders just because we felt the urge and curiosity, sometimes with limited pocket change and other times staying at five-star hotels. *Mami* still cringes and tries to hold us back out of fear for our safety. I, on the other hand, cover each new ground by thinking of *Papi* waving to me from the waterfalls. Whether it's a 50-mile bike ride in Mexico or getting lost in the Grand Palace in Bangkok, I always think of my times on the road with *la familia*.[17] I only hope our children will be as adventurous and fortunate to experience uncovered grounds with their own perspective.

[17] *The Family.*

Chapter Eight

Las Tías

Being part of a Mexican family often consists of building close relationships with your extended family. Once we moved from South Texas to Southern California, our parents hosted many of their younger siblings for long periods of time. I am sure my mother underestimated the family visits and the durations. I have come to the conclusion that my parents left the small town of Brownsville for more than just better opportunities. It's an unspoken truth that the two sides of the family didn't really get along. I have only heard rumors of the cause of their dislikes, but to tell you the truth, it just comes down to my aunts and mother being very strong and controlling women. You can never have too many of them in the same room without feeling some tension in the air.

Las Tías Garcías[18] are a vivid part of our childhood. In fact, many times they were our playmates, and we grew to admire them dearly. Yoli is the eldest of my father's four sisters. Lana is the youngest, my father being over ten years older than her. I'm not sure of all their ages, but it really doesn't matter because to us they have always been our *Tías*. I don't think they ever age, but just acquire husbands and children. Our *Tía* Vero is our single aunt who was born after Yoli, and is known to us as the traveler. We often live life vicariously through her adventures. Between Vero and Lana is Luisa. I seem to have a spiritual connection with her. I don't think she realizes how much I admire her, but one day I hope to compare our life stories.

---

[18] *My Aunts from my Father's side, the García Familiy.*

Our *Tías* lived with us occasionally through the years. I think they must have done it to antagonize my mother and to remain a part of their big brother's life. My parents made it a requirement for them to serve as our live-in babysitters during their visits. My *Tías* would often find amusement in making us do crazy human tricks such as stuffing as many marshmallows or grapes in our mouths as possible. We even had food eating contests to see who would be the prettiest princess in the whole wide world. Suzanne would often win in these events. She was quite vain as a child and was quick to devour entire bananas or cheeseburgers just to obtain the title. My aunts knew she would do this, so they would often use it to their advantage when they were tired of waiting for us to finish our happy meals at McDonald's. Among the pranks played, we would have the occasional never-ending hug or girly make-up sessions that made us wish to be just like our *Tías* when we grew up—as brave as Yoli, as sophisticated as Vero, as fun-loving as Luisa, and beautiful like Lana.

One evening my parents went out with our Uncle Rubén and Aunt Mari while our aunts promised to stay home and baby-sit our cousin and us. Being as young as they were, our *Tías* would allow us to do stuff out of the ordinary like watch scary movies and eat junk food. We had just finished watching one scary movie and started the second one when he heard a knock at the front door. We hadn't noticed that Yoli was no longer in the living room with us. Vero and Luisa squirmed to answer the door, but said they were scared. We were confused about their fear, but since they were scared and they were the grown-ups, it just came natural for us to be scared too.

My aunt Luisa was huddling with us while we yelped and squealed with laughter.

Las Niñas

"No Vero, don't answer the door, what if it's the boogie man!" I said.

"Oh, I don't think it's the boogie man, you girls are silly!" Vero responded. Luisa encouraged us to embrace each other and squeal together. Vero tiptoed towards the door and slowly turned the knob. As she pulled the door open, she peeked out to greet our unknown visitor. She flung open the door and screamed, "No! Don't take the girls!" A rather large creature entered the doorway wearing army green clothing, and black lace up boots. Its face reminded me of an alien with big dark eyes and a green hose as its nose. It was moving slowly towards us, arms extended in our direction. It was beyond anything we had seen in the movies.

"*Las Niñas*, I want the girls!" the thing grunted. All of us screamed with the utmost fear, and Cathy was crying hysterically. The four of us were clawing Luisa and tumbling over her. Tía Vero was laughing with her palm over her mouth. We felt overwhelmed by the creature that was inching its way towards us. Cathy was now whaling and the rest of us started to cry too. Our aunts started to console us.

"Girls, girls, it's not a monster. We're just playing, look its just Yoli." Vero said. Our faces were covered in tears and my vision was too blurry to even look their way. We all huddled together and cried. I think the joke was now on them. Unfortunately, we were all quite traumatized and crying profusely. They had to go through great lengths to dry up our tears and bring our focus to something else. Yoli started to remove her Marine fatigues and the gas mask that served as the intruder's face. We continued to cry and pleaded for our parents to come home. The crying lasted for quite some time, and we never finished watching the second movie. Our *Tías* tried to bribe our tears away with more cookies and soda. We turned down everything and continued to ask for our parents. We were all very scared and no longer felt safe with our *Tías*.

With time, we would put that memory aside and focus on the next one, as children often do. The weeks that followed were nerve wrecking for our *Tías* because they were waiting for the moment we would tell our parents. Some of us were having nightmares and our parents had no explanation for the incidents. Cathy was so traumatized she started sleeping with her parents again. I'm not sure if anyone ever told our parents, but through the years we made several references to that night. Our aunts still laugh about it. Yoli regretted it, especially after she realized how it affected Cathy.

We still find ourselves calling them for advice and joking with them as if we were children. I think once a person makes an impact in your life, you live in that moment for the rest of your life with them. Through the years, we have shared a number of memories, but somehow we still reflect on our dad in certain memories. None of us have ever stopped missing him and continue to include him in our lives. Now as an adult, I find myself reminiscing about my father with my aunts over a drink at a bar or while relaxing on South Padre Island during a visit. We like to exchange stories simply because we each have our own that the others haven't experienced. To me, *mis Tías*, my aunts will always be *Papi's* little sisters and I will always be the chubby, seven year old Sarita looking up to them. I guess the only difference now is that I have probably become more like them and can't help but express my own opinions, even when it causes us to grow apart. No matter the outcome, I am grateful to have strong women in my life. They have helped me become who I am and have given me the strength to

Las Niñas

stand up for myself. *¡Un abrazo y muchos besitos para mis Tías! Con Amor, Sarita.*[19]

---

[19] *A hug and a lot of kisses for my Aunts! Love, Sarita.*

Chapter Nine

Pecos River

As a child, each summer drive to Texas always felt longer than the last. Because of the various trips to visit our family, we had traditional landmarks that became part of our annual destination. Pecos River was one of our many pit stops on our way to Brownsville.

"*Papi* where are we now?" one of us would scream out from the back of the station wagon.

"We are close to Pecos River. Remember the river we always stop at?" he would reply. The Pecos River lies somewhere between New Mexico and Texas, but I'm not sure where. Nini always says that we should never look back at our childhood memories and try to relive them, because in the end, we will end up seeing things through an adult perspective, ruining its fairytale-like details.

"*Ay Rafa estamos todas greñudas*", as my mother would say "our hair is all messed up" - not easily translated but I am sure it gives an adequate description. My mother's objections never stopped my father from taking our picture. We were his girls and nothing would ever make us look or feel any less perfect than he made us out to be. My father enjoyed being our personal photographer, and always found the perfect location. That time, it was on a desolate rock sitting on the bank of the river. My mother griped all the way there as we walked through the loose gravel that lead to the riverbank. My father placed us on the rock as he created the perfect photo moment. He carried each one of us over the water while my mother envisioned us falling and being swept away by the river current. Can you imagine her crossing the river screaming after her babies? I'm sure the image crossed her mind.

The picture was finally taken as all three of us held on to my mother tightly and forced a smile for Papi. We climbed back up the riverside and laughed about the experience. We were always tempted to toss rocks back into the river. Mother childishly coaxed our father into admitting that she could throw farther than him. To prove her point, she threw one rock with all her might. She lost her balance on the gravel and slid down the riverbank. My father leaped to grab her, and they began laughing. It was the topic of conversation for miles, and each one of us repeated the adventure as if we hadn't seen it.

My family always managed to provide us with a family trip each year, even though sometimes it only consisted of a weekend trip to San Diego to visit Sea World. Whatever the event, we always seemed to enjoy the road trip more than anything else. We made the long drive to Dallas and Brownsville, Texas over many summers. Those summers were always consumed by quality time with our grandparents from both sides of the family. Although our parents chose to move away from their families, they still emphasized the importance of keeping a relationship with them. I can't imagine what we would have lost if we would have flown instead. A couple of hours on a plane wouldn't have provided us with the memories created on the three days of driving. I'm sure my mother would have preferred those long drives to be shorter. I remember the gas station stops and stocking up on beef jerky, onion rings, and Hawaiian fruit punch. My favorite memory is the three of us lying down in the back of the station wagon, staring at the countless stars and waiting for a shooting star to appear so we could make a wish.

Now my only wish would be to have that moment again with my sisters. I have to admit, I don't think I could make the road trips now as an adult, simply because I don't have a family of my own to accompany me. Until then, I think a road trip would just make me too anxious. I would find myself anticipating the arrival and eager for the moment to be reminiscing with my mom and sisters.

Chapter Ten

Twinkie, La Perra

    I remember the first time I saw Twinkie. I was about five or six years old and she was tied to a rope being held by her owners as they walked past our house. I rushed to pet her and the people stopped in our front yard for us to play with her. My mom walked towards the puppy and the people asked if we wanted her. My mom immediately refused, but I pleaded to keep the puppy. My mother insisted that our father would kill her for letting us keep the dog,

    "*¡Papi me va matar! Ay niñas, tienen que ayudarme convencer a su Papi ahora. Papi* is going to kill me! Girls, you are going to have to help me convince your father now," she said.

    Twinkie was a Collie and Cocker Spaniel mix. I named her Twinkie because she had the same sandy brown color as the popular snack cake. Her mother was a beautiful collie that occasionally roamed our neighborhood. That evening when *Papi* arrived home, I hid in the backyard while *Mami* explained about the newest member of the family. *Papi* came storming out to the backyard, looking for Twinkie, yelling that he was going to return her.

    "No Papi, don't take her! I love Twinkie!" I cried in her defense. My father looked at me angrily and glanced back at my mother. Suzanne and Nini stood inside peering out through the window. Nini was too young to understand what was going on and Suzanne was too terrified of Twinkie to even care. My father scooped Twinkie up in his strong dark arms and stormed back into the house. I was running behind him crying and pleading with all my heart.

"¡*Por favor, Papi*, Please, Daddy!" I cried. He stopped in the living room and turned around to look at my mother and me. *Mami* hugged me and kept me from following *Papi* out the door. He yelled at my mother, saying it was all her fault for letting the dog into our home.

"You try saying no to her! Can't you see this dog makes your daughter happy? You tell her that she can't have it, since you think it's that easy!" she yelled back. I was frantically crying and struggling to take in breaths of air without choking.

"¡*Por favor Papi, yo la voy cuidar con todo mi corazón!* Please daddy I will take care of her with all my heart!" I cried. My father struggled to look away and with all his *machismo* pride, he threw Twinkie down and said *"¡Yo no voy a cuidar este animal, ustedes dos tienen que cuidarla, si no yo la regreso!* I am not going to take care of this animal, both of you will have to take care of her, if not I will return her!" Twinkie ran straight to me and I hugged her so hard she whimpered.

"¡*Gracias Papi, te quiero mucho*! Thank you daddy, I love you very much!" I said as I smiled at Mami. She remained quiet and waited for *Papi* to leave the room. As soon as he did, *Mami* made sure to state all the rules and reminded me that *Papi* would return her if we didn't take care of our new family member.

Twinkie became my best friend and I was the only kid in our neighborhood to have a dog. Twinkie became the neighborhood pet. There were many times that I found myself telling her stories. I had even planned to run away with her when I was mad at my parents, but since I didn't have any money to buy her food, I decided against the idea. Nini immediately became attached to Twinkie too, but Suzanne spent many backyard moments standing on a chair or table to avoid the ferocious animal tugging at her clothes to play. After some time, Twinkie won over Suzanne too and all of us played together. Twinkie became our regular playmate, and occasionally pretended to be a lion, shark, or horse and always begged for belly rubs.

Twinkie didn't get much bigger than a mid-size dog, but as they say a dog usually resembles its owner, so did Twinkie. She became a little husky since we generally fed her table food, especially heavy Mexican food. Through the years, Twinkie and I were known to be a little over-weight and were often placed on alternative diets. Every once in awhile, my parents would try to keep her on dog food, but she would easily outwit us by spending her evenings snapping at flies before even touching her food.

Twinkie was never really cared for medically, probably since we were a struggling family. My parents never really felt compelled to pay a visit to a veterinarian. Fortunately, Twinkie never got sick or hurt. She was never fixed either, so she did manage to get pregnant. One morning we found our father repairing the backyard gate. We inquired about it, and all he said was that some dog tried to get in to fight with Twinkie. We were under the impression that the dog never made it in, but the gate stated otherwise. Apparently, Twinkie was the beautiful blonde of the neighborhood and since she never left the backyard, she was also the forbidden fruit for the stray dogs. Somehow a neighborhood dog, heated by animalistic urges, gnawed his way through our gate and got Twinkie pregnant.

Sometime after that, my father announced that

Twinkie was going to have puppies. It was nature's way of introducing the "birds and the bees" to us. Through her pregnancy, our parents let us feel the puppies growing in her stomach. One early Saturday morning, our father woke us up and took us outside to witness childbirth from a dog's perspective. Instead of the enormous doghouse my father had built for Twinkie, she had chosen to give birth behind a rather large bush under my parent's bedroom window.

It was an incredible experience. We were all huddled around the bush in our pink nightgowns, staring with astonishment while a million questions ran through our minds. We all wanted to touch the puppies, but our father urged us not to. He said that we couldn't because the puppies had to keep their puppy scent for Twinkie to like them. Unfortunately, it started to rain and the puppies needed to be moved before a puddle formed in the small burrow Twinkie had made. *Papi* tried to have Twinkie move the puppies into the doghouse, and she eventually did, but one puppy was left behind and *Papi* had to pick up the puppy with his bare hands. It happened to be the runt of the litter and ended up being the puppy we had to feed and care for because Twinkie ended up rejecting him.

Being children, it was hard to understand why Twinkie would reject her own child, or why a father was not present to visit his puppies. This life experience provided us with many confusing conversations with our parents. Eventually the time came for our parents to explain that we couldn't keep all the puppies and that we must give them away. After accepting this, we started to find homes for the puppies. We made poster signs and hung them out at a major intersection as we stood next to them on a Saturday morning. Days later, with only two puppies left out of eight, an Asian family approached us. My father was speaking with them and offered them a puppy. I stood next to my father out of curiosity. The family started to ask about the mother of the puppies. I guessed they wanted to know what she looked liked. They insisted on knowing her weight and size and if we would consider selling her. To my surprise, *Papi* was very angry about the inquiry and stated with great force that our pet was not for sale and then he refused to give them any of the puppies. I was a little surprised that he didn't give away a puppy since he was pretty adamant about not keeping any of them.

Later he explained that they were Vietnamese and wanted Twinkie so they could eat her for dinner. They explained to my father that dogs taste best after they give birth, since the meat was still very tender. I was disgusted by the fact that people would actually consider eating our pet. *Papi* had to explain to us that different cultures have different traditions and even though he got angry with the Vietnamese man, he told us that we shouldn't be angry with the man for wanting to eat a his own type of food, "Just like we eat *barbacoa*, meat from a cows head," he said. We managed to find suitable homes for the remaining puppies and I vowed to never let anyone eat Twinkie.

That's how we were raised, to respect others beliefs and lives. It shouldn't go without saying that it took us awhile to figure out we were different ourselves. The first time I realized I was not like everyone else was the day I took a *burrito* to school for lunch. I remember looking around and seeing that only two of us had the same type of food. Everyone else had sandwiches. I noticed that they had white bread and other stuff inside that I was not familiar with. They even had the chips that were too expensive to buy in the stores. At the Mexican Mercado we only got tortilla chips or *chicharrones* to have with *salsa*. It wasn't that I didn't like my *burrito*, it was just that some of the kids stared at it and asked me what it had in it. For some reason, beans are hard to describe to white kids. Now remember, it was before the Taco Bell boom, back in the late seventies, early eighties. Today, I would love to have someone make me *burritos* for lunch and everyone around me would kill for a homemade *carne asada burrito*, hell people pay top dollar for them now. Back then it was hard to be different, especially when you didn't know you actually were. Twinkie not only exposed us to all kinds of experiences, but also to the acceptance of others.

Chapter Eleven

Mi Primera y Última Comunión...

My First Communion was one of the first introductions to the Catholic religion that I experienced. I was baptized into the catholic faith as an infant, and at the age of nine I received the sacraments of penance and Eucharist all in the same week. I looked forward to being able to walk up to the altar to take the body of Christ, as everyone older than me did. What intimidated me the most was confessing all my sins in person to a priest days before the formal ceremony. The first confession had to be done face-to-face instead of in a confessional booth.

Prior to that day, punishment for my behavior meant being sent to my room or being spanked with Mami's *chancla*, which was comparable to a house slipper. I had to face whatever the Father provided me with for penance. It was just as confusing as the punishment from my parents because each outcome could be completely different from the previous one. There were times when my mom didn't spank us for not cleaning our rooms, and then there were times she screamed at us and chased us throughout the house with the *chancla*. Sometimes it was even left for *Papi* to deal with when he came home, which also transpired to different outcomes each time. I made it through my first confession with a couple of Our Fathers and Hail Mary's. It was easy enough that I would trade it for the *chancla* any day. After that, I was ready for my first communion.

The preparation started the night before the actual event. My mother rolled my hair in curlers, and decided to use perm rods for my bangs because she swore the curls would look better and last throughout the entire day. My godmother made me a special dress for the occasion. I'm sure my parents saw this as another stepping-stone in my life. If we only have known then, what we know now, it probably would've been seen as my last white dress event. I guess we should have taken more pictures.

As coincidental as it may seem, I chose my godparents Connie and Tom because they were our closest friends from church. I soon found out that my baptism godparents, whom I never really knew, were also named Connie and Tom. Unfortunately, both sets of godparents disappeared from my life sometime after the religious proceedings due to our family relocating.

As bedtime moved closer, my excitement grew, reminding me of the nights before going to Disneyland. The next morning, I woke up earlier than usual. I'm not sure if it was due to being too excited, or if it was the fact that by morning my head felt like it was going to fall off because of the heavy curlers weighing it down.

I started my first communion day by eating cereal with Suzanne and Nini. The three of us were still in our pajamas and I still have the very tight curlers decorating my head. I remember Suzanne asking me why I needed to talk to Father William before I took my first communion. I explained that everybody had to confess, not just me.

"Did you tell him that you hit me?" she asked bitterly.

"That's not a sin," I said.

"Uh, uh! They said you have to tell God all your bad things so you can go to heaven," she said in reply.

"I know, I'm making my first communion, not

you!" I yelled back. Suddenly, my parents walked in and asked us about our conversation. Suzanne repeated her comments and *Mami* said *"Claro que sí, pero Susan tú también vas a tener que decirles de todas las cosas que le haces a Nini* – Of course, but Suzanne you will have also have to tell them of the things you do to Nini."

"Yeah, but not now, next year," Suzanne replied. Both of my parents started laughing and hurried us to get ready for church.

Many of our childhood Sunday mornings were not much different from that one. Prior to my father's death, we were very religious. Of course, us girls didn't have a choice, but it never crossed our mind to question the tradition or our beliefs. All of our friends were at church, and we prayed to be chosen as the family to bring up the wine and Eucharist to the altar for blessing. We always attended catechism classes and our parents participated in several church groups, including the Spanish mass choir. Being Catholic was as much a part of our life as being Mexican. It was part of our culture. *Mi primera comunión*[20] was the first religious tradition that I led my sisters through.

As my mother removed the perm rods from my hair, we both gasped in disappointment. My curls were so tightly spun that they looked like tiny, coiled snakes on my head. *Mami* attempted to loosen the curls by pulling on them, but they just recoiled and frizzed out. By the third try, the top of my head reminded me of a Chia pet. I naturally started to cry, and *Mami* reassured me that she could fix my hair. She washed out my bangs and brought out the veil to sit on the cushion we had created for it.

[20] *My First Communion, a Catholic Sacrament.*

The next thing I remembered was walking towards the church in two lines. The boys were dressed in pressed suits and the girls were dressed in white. All of us held our palms together as we often did while praying before bedtime. I was eager to look over to see who would walk me into the church; I guess I was also envisioning this day as a future wedding celebration. I saw a boy I had a crush on looking over at me. I saw him look at my hair and smile. One of the nuns scolded us to walk in a straight line and face forward. Looking back, she was probably addressing all the kids, not me in particular. Everyone was waving to friends and family, posing for pictures, and fidgeting with their special attire.

I wish I could remember more about the ritual, but in all honesty, I remember very little of the actual mass. All I know is that candles and individual blessings were involved. I do remember that the young deacon of our parish had recently been ordained a priest and we were the subjects of his first ceremony. The only reason that moment stood out for me was because Father Jaime played an important role in the years we shared with the parish. He participated in several of our family's religious sacraments, performing the mass when our parents renewed their vows, and participated in *Papi's* funeral ceremony. He was more than our priest. He attended our family gatherings, drank beer with the men, and even mourned in our time of sorrow.

In addition to Father Jaime's involvement, I remember the *pan dulce* and *atole* we shared after mass. *Mami* had arranged for us to celebrate my newly obtained sacrament through the traditional custom of eating Mexican sweet bread and toasting with the ever so sweet, thick milk drink. We invited friends and family who expressed their appreciation by providing gifts, most with religious sentiment. As

Las Niñas

usual, the event concluded with more food, drinks, and music. By the end of the night, I had forgotten about the bad hair day and refused to put up my white dress until bedtime. The dress was made to only wear once, similar to a *quinceañera*[21] or wedding.

Throughout our childhood, our family life revolved around Catholicism and our church. We attended our church's Catholic school for three years, as well as an associated Catholic ballet academy. Both were located in a semi-bad neighborhood caught between Mexican gang boundaries in Santa Ana, California. At the time, religion probably kept most of the adolescents in our school and congregation out of gangs. As soon as we found a reason to disengage from the church, some of us fell into the other types of groups.

After my father passed away, I found it really hard to turn to God or to the church. It became even worse when my mother relocated us to a new neighborhood and we stopped attending mass. At the time, I was dating a boy from the Catholic school who was facing changes of his own. What I lacked in my own family, he had in his. What I had as an advantage in my new environment, he had as a disadvantage. Neither one of us could think positively enough to appreciate what we could bring together. After we left middle school, we faced going to high schools in completely different environments. He had to face a gang-infested neighborhood, because his home sat on the territorial border of two rival gangs. I had to deal with my father's death and the culture shock of a new neighborhood in which my ethnicity was definitely considered a minority.

[20] *A Mexican tradition similar to the "Sweet Sixteen," but a girl's "Fifteenth Birthday (formal) Party."*

The only thing we had that remained consistent was our relationship, which at that time, was not moving fast enough for him and much too fast for me.

As a result of our personal experiences, we both rebelled against God and our family in one way or another. Unfortunately, it took us through some very difficult years. He ended up with child and soon after, a wife at the age of nineteen. My path led me out of my mother's house and into working three jobs by my nineteenth birthday, while attempting to attend community college. Although I have often said religion is just a discipline, some people need it in their lives to maintain a civilized environment. I now believe that it's more than that. It provided me with a foundation for knowing what's right from wrong. I have been down many paths throughout my life, but I think the faith that I built in God in the first thirteen years allowed me to develop faith in myself for the last seventeen.

In a way, our lives are all a sort of religion, we establish our own bibles for others to interpret and use as guidance later or not. We plan our own rituals to observe at monumental times in our lives. My life is neither the holiest nor the most successful by another person's definition, but between God and me, I'm still that little girl in the white dress looking over my shoulder to see who is looking at me while I make my own path towards heaven. I may have stopped to wave or even gone the wrong way at times, but in the end I know God has been there all along listening to my confessions. I know he has forgiven me as I have learned to forgive myself.

Chapter Twelve

Plum, Plums and more Plums!

Growing up in Santa Ana, California was quite a unique experience for us. I can't say that many people would agree, simply because parts of it are now known as lower class neighborhoods striving to keep the gangs away from their homes. As children, we were very oblivious to the nearby "hooker" boulevard and the teenage boys smoking pot in the ditch located behind our backyard. At the time, the neighborhood exposed us to a historical background of Southern California. Santa Ana was once filled with fields of fruit and migrant workers from Mexico.

Through the years, the plum tree in our backyard provided my sisters and I with plenty of entertainment. Each year, we eagerly waited for the plums to grow and then spent days examining them to make sure they were ready for picking. Our parents were very particular about picking them at the right moment, because for some reason they had us convinced that it would be deadly if we ate them while they were still green. That was the threat they used to keep us from picking them prematurely.

On one particular afternoon, our uncle Ramón was watching us while our parents were out. We always kept ourselves pretty entertained, which was fairly easy since there were three of us. The backyard was enormous in our eyes and had everything we could ever want. We had a swing set, our own dog, and many flowers and plants to keep our vivid imaginations active. Many times we were in a fairytale forest or a scary jungle with wild animals. I am not sure which setting we might had chosen on that particular day, but we were prancing around and chasing each other as we often did. The fun times led up to Suzanne falling.

"Aah, I hurt myself!" Suzanne shouted. Nini and I started laughing.

"It's not funny! Stop laughing, it's all your fault! I'm going to tell!" she said as tears fell down her face.

"No, it's not!" I shouted back. "I didn't push you!"

"Yeah, but you made me run after you and Nini. I didn't want to be "it" this time!" she cried.

"You never want to be it!" I replied, while Nini watched quietly. She seemed to be used to our quarrels by now. Suzanne refused to get up and continued whining to us, and then as if the world had come to a complete slow pace, she shouted with pure hatred "You are so fat!" I have to admit I was a pretty pudgy child, but at the time it was definitely a sore topic to bring up. Suzanne would use her harshest words when she found herself defeated. As soon as the words were spat out, Nini's eyes grew with fear and Suzanne sat with a furious look challenging whatever actions were destined to follow her crude comment. The depiction of this memory may be a little biased, and I still find myself overly concerned about my weight, even though I'm at a steady 125 pounds and 5'2" and a half in height. I can't say I am sharing this with any regret, but it's definitely filled with pure amusement.

As the words slowly buried themselves in my mind, I looked down at my little belly hanging out of my pink shirt and tightly fitted red and white striped shorts, and saw a rotten plum lying next to my feet. It was the perfect time to pick plums now, but we obviously could not pick them fast enough and our

Las Niñas

backyard became a plum field. I did what every other fat kid at the age of nine would do, I bent over slowly, picked up the plum, and held it over my head as a threat. Suzanne didn't flinch. She sat there and filled her face with air only to mimic my expression. The catholic guilt set in, and I made the quick decision to purposely not hit her with it, but rather just throw it to give her a good scare.

I'm not sure what happened, next but the scene seemed to have switched to fast forward. The plum went flying in the air and smacked Suzanne right in her left eye. As it landed, red plum juice oozed out and showered her face. She took those perfectly air-filled cheeks of hers and blew out an excruciating scream. She stood up and paced around screaming and holding her hands over her eye. What came next was one of the funniest moments in our childhood. Suzanne pulled her hands away and looked down to find red plum juice coloring her skin. She immediately went from the winy kid to the franticly crying little girl.

"I'm bleeding, I'm bleeding!" she yelled, running directly to my uncle, who at no time felt the need to prevent this situation. He looked at her and could not control his laughter. Nini and I followed his lead. Suzanne was really under the impression that her eye was bleeding, and as the big sister, I was compelled to squeeze out some words of sympathy.

"You are not bleeding, its plum juice!" I said, trying to stifle my laughter. "No, it's not!" she said, tasting her finger. She immediately filled her hands with rotten plums in retaliation and the chase continued!

That's how our arguments went. We never ceased to interact or stop talking to each other as some siblings do. We just moved on to the next moment, whether it was sharing a meal or just watching TV together. Now don't get me wrong, there were some moments that we exchanged many mean comments and some led up to physical contact, but we never forgot that we were unconditional playmates. Our parents made sure to remind us that we had to stick together.

"Tus hermanas son las únicas amigas que vas tener por toda tu vida – Your sisters are the only friends you will have throughout your whole life," they always said. Even now as adults we have had some heated spats that have led to sudden hang-ups or unwanted confrontations, but we still manage to talk through them and settle our differences. With time we know that where we reside, husbands and children will become individual priorities, but they will not keep us from or replace our relationship as sisters. My sisters and I have more than a friendship; we have an unconditional bond with each other that we are devoted to through eternity.

Chapter Thirteen

Once upon a bedtime...

Once at bedtime, *Papi y Mami* were chasing my sisters and me through the house trying to persuade us to get ready for bed. I had requested a bedtime snack while Nini was pleading with *Mami* to let her skip her daily bath. Amusingly, Suzanne was parading naked in the hallway after pouring massive amounts of Mr. Bubbles in the running water.

Bedtime was tough for all of us because we never really had a routine. *Papi's* shifts at work would change every so often and Mami's mood would fluctuate from one moment to the next. *Mami* would either use playful games for persuasion or threaten us with *La Chancla*.[22] In addition to these inconsistencies, I can't help but mention the random long-term houseguests we endured throughout the years that kept our immediate family life chaotic as well. There were periods where we all had our own rooms and times the three of us had to sleep on the same bed. Bedtime was always somewhere between eight o'clock and whenever the rest of the household settled down.

As most other children, we found ways to defy all of the rules at bedtime. Our tactics only delayed the event, but never dismissed it. Sometimes we would just hide under a bed and draw pictures on the box spring or simply fall asleep in random locations. After several unsuccessful attempts to establish a routine, our parents strategically coordinated a bedtime that would entice all three of us.

---

[22] *House slipper, or flip-flop, which was often used to spank a child's bottom.*

We would take a bath, get in our pajamas, and line up at the big living room window in time to watch the Disneyland fireworks that showered over our neighborhood around seven thirty in the evening.

Living in Santa Ana had one distinctive advantage; it was next to Anaheim, the home of Disneyland. Somehow our family always managed an annual trip to the famous amusement park. We always looked forward to those days at Disney. We overlooked the early wake ups, packing homemade snacks, and wearing matching outfits, as long as it meant we were headed to Disneyland for the day. The outing became an annual family tradition. When other family members came to visit, we knew that we would be going back to visit Disneyland. Upon their arrival, we greeted our guests with lots of hugs and cheers, unknowingly thanking them ahead of time for the opportunity to visit all our favorite Disney characters again.

If I had to choose one of the many Disney memories to relive, it would definitely be *Abuela's*[23] story. One particular summer we had a Bustamante family reunion. Everyone from my mother's side attended, except for our cousin Cathy and her parents. Over that summer, they were munching on sauerkraut and sausages while enduring their four-year residency with the Air force in Germany.

We had spent most of the day at Disneyland making our way through our favorite rides—Pirates of the Caribbean, Haunted House and It's a Small World. We had the time to squeeze in one more ride before eating a late lunch, and we chose Space Mountain, because of the high-speed roller coaster turns. As is the case with most popular rides, the line was extremely long.

---

[23] *Grandmother's.*

Las Niñas

Everyone stood in the line together and waited. A couple of exits prior to boarding, most of the adults left with exception of my Father and Uncle Javier. They seemed to be the thrill seekers in the adult group. My Mother hates that because my Father had a heart problem and the warning signs for these types of rides always recommended that people with heart problems not ride. Neither my mother nor the warnings stopped him from boarding the rides.

Throughout the day we would ask our grandmother if she was going on the ride too.

"*¿Por qué me preguntas, crees que soy vieja o qué?* Why do you ask, do you think I'm old or what?" she always responded. My mother firmly stated that grandma was not getting on Space Mountain.

"*¡Ahora tú me estás llamando vieja también!* Now you are calling me old too!" Grandma replied. As the line progressed, Grandma insisted that she was boarding. About half way through the one-hour line, Grandma spotted an elderly couple standing in line with their grandson. She pointed them out to us and said "*¿A poco creen que soy más vieja que ellos?* Do you really believe I'm older than that couple over there?" We denied the fact that she was old and continued to describe the ride to her. When we got to the first exit, we all insisted that Grandma should leave too. My mother decided to play a trick on grandma.

"*Ay, niñas, dejen que su abuela se suba, pero no pueden decir que no le avisamos,* Ah girls, let your grandma board, but she can't say we didn't warn her," she said. Grandma again pointed out the elderly couple and stuck to her decision. What she didn't notice was that the couple never boarded, they simply walked through the seats to exit before the roller coaster disembarked from the boarding tracks. As everyone settled in the seats, all the children kept an eye on *Abuela*. We giggled as the shoulder restraints lowered, and we squirmed in our seats with anticipation. The coaster slowly rolled into a dark tunnel with thousands of little lights that created the illusion of outer space.

The ride started with slow trek up a steep slope leading into a fast plunge into an abyss of darkness, which culminated with *Abuela* letting out endless stream of Spanish profanities. We all giggled at each turn and plunge, while *Abuela* continued to educate us on all the proper pronunciation of the short-term lingo that she had raised us to believe were harmless words used to express anger. Most vividly remembered was the word "*Chingado*"[24] which was previously mentioned in our lives as "Chin" or "Chihuahua" and usually prefaced with "*Ay*" and followed with a person's name. *Abuela* always seemed a little different in comparison to most grandmothers. She smoked, drank, and now openly cursed. Somewhere beneath the knitted pink sweater and over-sized clothes was an aggressive, rebellious woman who had obviously been around the block enough times to learn all the proper curse words. Once the ride came to a complete stop, *Abuela* loudly commented *"¡Creo que me meé in mis calzones en el Espace Montaña!* I think I peed in my underwear in Space Mountain!" She broke out in a hysterical laughter. Once we met up with the rest of our group, we couldn't help but retell our story to anyone willing to listen. That's how we acquired our Disney moments, not as classical as the ones shared by Walt, but definitely colorful. ¡*Ay Chingado*, it's *de* end!

[24] *Spanish bad word for completely messed up or F%#ked!*

Chapter Fourteen

Alice Monique

"¡*Abre la puerta, Juana!*" My grandmother screamed at the bathroom door. The door had been locked for over an hour and my *Tía* Juanita had been complaining of stomach pains for a while prior to locking herself in the small bathroom. After several excruciating screams from Juanita, *mi Abuela's* anger shifted to a mother's panic. She contacted my mother in California, and my mother advised her to call the emergency number. Juanita had been pregnant and didn't tell anybody. She was sixteen and lived in Brownsville, Texas. She was giving birth to her premature daughter in the bathroom. Once the paramedics arrived, they broke down the door and found my aunt bent over the toilet while the baby's crown was visible from the birth canal. The baby dying in route to the hospital, but her angels in disguise brought her back into this world.

That's how Alice Monique became part of our family. Hardly alive and saved by complete strangers. She even made the local newspapers before she was even held by her own mother. I can't imagine what *Tía* Juana was thinking at the time, but I can only assume that our Mexican culture and the small town's social norms did not make her feel comfortable enough to seek help.

Brownsville, Texas is a small city located on the southern-most tip of Texas. I always like to say being born in Brownsville is the closest you can get to be a real Mexican. In fact, it offers the best of both worlds—all the Mexican heritage with the rights of an American citizen. Of course, it has disadvantages, such as the small town mentality and being banished from greater opportunities available in bigger and more diverse environments. I have heard from Brownsville locals that it's easy to get stuck in Brownsville simply because of family. Growing up in that area just makes everything else seem too foreign and distant from what is known as home. I have never minded visiting Brownsville because I didn't grow up there and to me it represents *la familia*, home-cooked flour tortillas, South Padre Island, and now *Papi's* burial place.

Juana is the second youngest of seven children, and the second daughter out of three. The first daughter was my mother. *Tía* Juana, who now goes by Janie, is only six years older than me, so we grew up close to each other. Juana and her younger sister, Carmen, had a better relationship with each other than with my mother, but I can't imagine being raised by a woman that was twice a widow and very cold due to her own personal struggles in life. *Abuela* tried her best, and our generation has definitely benefited from our family's experiences.

Juana gave birth to Alice Monique on July 7th, 1985. All we ever knew about Monique's father was that he was much older than Juana, about eight years older. *Mi abuela* was desperate to prosecute for statutory rape, which was actively supported in Texas. Juana did not need to consent to the charges since she was under age. It would be her mother and proud older brothers who would make this man face his consequences. Due to her so-called devotion, Juana refused to expose him, and the case remained open for five years. Apparently, she had shared the information with our *Tío* Ramón. We found out when he brought the man home after running into him at a grocery store in Dallas in 2003. At the age of eighteen, Monique's father entered her life and it couldn't have occurred at a better time.

Juanita's pregnancy and her baby's birth were a major disappointment to the older siblings. Our family never really openly discussed the issues. It was like everything else that we should have talked about in our family, such as sex, drugs, Grandma's affair with little Carmelita's father, *Tía* Carmen's brutal death, my parent's marital problems, everything that had some negative impact. When I reflect on Juana's life, I have to say it definitely served its purpose in our family, by exposing the next generation to a situation we would have been immune to.

Some months after the birth, Juana and her child were furiously swept away to California. She had lived with us for a year. My parents opened their home to offer them opportunities that did not exist in Brownsville at the time. Juana attended a teenage parent high school that provided daycare and a regular high school schedule. It was a state funded school that only required Juana to spend her lunch breaks with her daughter in exchange for the convenience. We loved having Monique around. We had many days in which we were preoccupied playing with our little Monique. Many times we treated her just like a doll, dressed her up, made baby talk, fed her, and pretended she was ours to keep.

We often heard our parents comment on Monique's motor skills, and how she was so advanced for her age, especially since she was born premature. Monique learned to crawl pretty early and many times we would find her crawling on the bedroom floor after she had been laid to sleep on the bed. We never found her crying, so we assumed she had arrived on the floor safely. One day, Juana found her clinging to the bed's comforter and sliding down to the floor.

I think it's quite interesting to hear stories of your

childhood, especially the ones you can't really remember. A memory that we've always shared with Monique is the time Suzanne and I dropped her on the floor.

The three of us would often take on many of the parenting responsibilities such as changing diapers, bathing and feeding Monique. We had many heated discussions about who could actually do what. On one occasion, Suzanne and I found Monique awake in her crib and we both wanted to carry her. I wouldn't doubt it if we purposely woke her up just to hold her. I had her in my arms when Suzanne began to grab her from me. I insisted that she was too young to carry Monique. Neither one of us was willing to let go, and the argument developed into a tug of war. Our fight escalated and caught Juana's attention. She barged into the room and yelled at us to let Monique go. I'm not sure what happened next, but I guess her yelling scared us into doing just that. We both let go of Monique and she fell to the ground and began to scream. My parents ran into the room and found all four of us crying together. Juana was crying because her baby was dropped, and we were crying because we dropped her. We were sent to our rooms and strict rules were set after that, and we were no longer allowed to carry her unless supervised by our parents.

My father accepted Monique as one of his own and cared for her as he had cared for us. Monique's *Papi* was our *Papi* and no one would have it any other way. My mother was the overly concerned older sister who vented her disappointment by criticizing and correcting Juana's parenting skills. The arguments between them would often lead to Juana slamming her bedroom door and refusing to come out. My father would try to intervene, but it was nearly impossible with their tempers. During one argument, I overheard my aunt accuse my mother of abandoning her by

Las Niñas

leaving for California.

The final argument happened after my parents sat down with Juana to talk about adopting Monique. They presented it as an opportunity for Juana to continue with her education in Texas or California without having to worry about her daughter. They promised to return Monique once she was settled, and offered long summers for visitation. I can't imagine a more devastating proposal than to be asked to give up your only reason for living. Soon after that discussion, Juana packed her bags and returned to Texas with her daughter.

Monique is now the eldest of three children and a sophomore in college. She received a partial scholarship to a major university after many years as an honor roll student. Her father is providing the unconditional support he denied her earlier in life, and has offered Monique the opportunity to focus on school without having to work. She aspires to be a speech pathologist and is looking forward to being a mother one day, but only after she achieves her life goals. Monique is definitely smarter than most of us on the relationship side of things too. That's how Alice Monique has chosen to live her life and contribute to our family.

It's amazing how some lessons in life must be learned through great struggles. I can't say I know exactly how Monique feels because we are quite distant in age, but I can imagine what keeps her motivated everyday to pursue her life goals. The younger set of first born Mexican-Americans in our family are all quite diverse and have been able to take our family one step further in life.

My sisters and I learned many life lessons from my father's death, but the last lesson he taught us was the importance of education and setting goals. I received my first set of bad grades in eighth grade. They included a "C," "D" and "F" on one report card. My father was so disappointed, and it was the first time I saw him cry. He did not confront me about it until some weeks later. The same week he went into the hospital, I received a letter in the mail. A letter that explained his whole life in four pages filled with writing on both sides, ultimately expressed the importance of education. In the letter, he wrote that each generation is given more opportunities, and therefore should make an attempt to accomplish ten times more than the last. For our generation, this meant graduating from high school and attending college. I shared this letter with both of my sisters after his death, and all of us use his words to remind us of our parent's purpose in life.

Since then, Suzanne and my cousin Vanessa have received graduate degrees from top universities in the nation. I lived in China for eighteen months, and Nini is currently self-employed and happily married to a wonderful man. They are expecting my parent's first grandchild who is to be named Rafael, after *Papi*.

For the younger cousins in my family, the better opportunities now mean attending better universities and possibly graduate programs. I am proud to say I have two female cousins attending nursing programs; another one is a graduate of an east coast university who was awarded a full scholarship and is now a female officer in the Marines. Another cousin is in the Air force Academy in Colorado after being accepted to several military schools and competing in several marathons. A male cousin is studying Chinese while living in the crowded streets of Beijing at the age of twenty-one, and a fifth one is attending a private Catholic university and is studying international business. The eldest of the bunch has just finished a tour with the Peace Corps and is living

Las Niñas

in Thailand as an English teacher, while one of my youngest male cousins has been recognized as a war hero. Our youngest female cousin is enjoying life and moving away from home for the first time.

Even after all these admirable experiences, we still anxiously wait to see yet another cousin take us even further. It's hard to imagine that it all started within a lifetime. Our grandparents filled out applications to enter America, which gave their grandchildren an opportunity to fill out college applications that will eventually help their own grandchildren in the future. After all, that's our duty as new Americans, we must repay our family for their sacrifices and struggles with success, because it wouldn't be worth it otherwise.

Chapter Fifteen

¡La Gran Fiesta!

Anyone that has ever spent a birthday with me as an adult has experienced my event planning skills that always allow me to be the center of attention on my special day. I usually start planning my own celebration before anyone else can even acknowledge that my birthday is nearby. It tends to frustrate my friends, especially those that have been around for a while. Most of them have succumbed to asking me what day they should reserve for the party instead of organizing anything on their own. I only had one surprise party hosted by a previous boyfriend and my good friend, Yvette. I overheard the planning and gave them the opportunity to run the show that year. I tend to describe my birthday as the biggest holiday in the year, next to Christmas, of course.

My birthday has always been well celebrated. Being the first grandchild has provided me with an over abundance of attention. My first birthday was a prime example. I have many pictures showing almost every minute of that event. It took place at a neighborhood park in Brownsville, Texas, and I wore an aquamarine-blue, puffy dress decorated with fine lace at its edges and dolled up with a matching ribbon. I was dressed from head to toe with frilly accessories. I would almost compare my dress to the tacky bridesmaid dresses you encounter at second-hand clothing stores. From what was captured in the pictures, the festivities consisted of the park's designated area being decorated with streamers and balloons. The decorations were accompanied by two rather large *piñatas*, a cake with an elephant toy, and about fifty of my closest friends and family. Not my

Las Niñas

personal friends, but my parents and grandparents invited their friends, their children and, for some, their children's children to celebrate *"la gran fiesta*[25]*."*

Whether it was a birthday, baptism, or first communion, all of them gave our family an excuse to throw a bar-B-Q or large gathering of some sort. I was not capable of hitting a *piñata*, much less gathering the candy that came out of it. By the end of the event, I was only wearing a saggy diaper, and a gold necklace was dangling over my little belly and a matching bracelet was hanging from my wrist. My first birthday consisted of tasting cake for the first time and being carried and entertained by various family members. The adult festivities included eating *carne asada*[26] and telling countless stories while sipping on a *cerveza con sal y limón.*[27]

Suzanne was born one year and one week later. My second birthday was not as festive as the first because my mother was about to give birth to my little sister. My first birthday party was the only one during my childhood that was focused solely on me. Suzanne and I shared all of our childhood birthday celebrations until my thirteenth birthday. I only stopped having them because I was being rebellious and refused to participate in any family gatherings.

My event planning skills were developed after many years of being coached by my mother. She was so detailed that she would find matching outfits for Suzanne and I to wear for our party.

[25] *The Great Party.*

[26] *Grilled flank steak.*

[27] *Beer with salt and lime.*

It would only confuse some of our guests into thinking were we twins. At cake time, the doubts were settled once the two sets of numbers were placed on the full-sheet cake that took up the center of the table. My mother took pride in her events because she also planned her own attire perfectly, as if to give off the notion that someone else did all the hard work while she sat and looked pretty. I think she did it just to be able to announce proudly *"Claro que hice todo yo misma, menos la carne asada, eso se lo dejo a Rafa, así tiene algo que hacer –* Of course I did everything myself, except for the grilling, I leave that for Rafa, that way he has something to do."

La gran fiesta usually required two weeks of preparation. The first task was to search for the *piñata*. This process usually included a trip to the Mexican market after mass on Sunday, or a quick run across the Tijuana border. The excursion depended on the size of the party and the type of *piñata* we wanted. As the event grew closer, my parents would skim through the advertisements in the newspaper for specials on chips, soda, and beer. Sometimes we would visit two different grocery stores in one day just to save some money on the dozens of cases of beverages we would have for our guests.

During our visit to the *Carnicería* (Mexican meat market), my father would pick out the best *fajitas* (skirt meat) and chicken pieces. These were the most important items for the event, next to the *pastel y piñata*. The grill was creatively organized by sections of chicken, beef, and green onions. *Papi* would marinate the chicken in a mixture of pineapple, orange, and lime. *La carne asada* would be prepared the morning of the party in various spices and lots of lime and *cerveza* for tenderizing.

Mami would make her infamous Mexican rice,

Las Niñas

salsa, frijoles borrachos[28] and potato salad. You don't have to be Mexican to experience this tradition. Texan's have brisket, pork ribs and sausage and most Americans grill burgers and hot dogs. Through the years our family acquired all three types of grilling, sometimes all at the same event.

Las Tías[29], my father's sisters that now lived in Oceanside, always arrived early carrying some sort of dish and rolling up their sleeves to help in the kitchen. My sisters and I could be seen running around cleaning the backyard or getting ready. Twinkie, our dog, always sensed a party arriving when the grill was being sparked up and the coolers containing the various drinks were being set outside along the extra patio furniture that consisted of plastic chairs and tables. The preparation would make her run around and bark at us.

La gran fiesta was coming together. Suzanne and I got our hair combed in the living room while the guests began to arrive. A table was set aside for gifts. An envelope meant the possibility of money, medium size rectangle boxes were my favorites, and all the rest were surprises. Sometimes we would find gifts with both of our names on them. Those were highly disliked because after the guests departed, *Papi* y *Mami* would divide the pile equally among both of us to prevent any disputes. When we did receive an odd number of them, we would give one to Nini as a consolation prize for not being born the same month as us. She always got yipped on the gifts since her birthday fell right after Christmas.

[28] *Translates to "drunken beans," Pinto bean soup made with beer.*
[29] *The aunts.*

We entertained *nuestros amigos y familia*[30] with *Rancheras* (Spanish country music), *piñatas*, and lots of food y *cerveza*.

The piñata was always the highlight of the party. By then, the kids had become anxious while some of the parents seemed too happy from the beers. The younger children always went first and never had to be blindfolded. The older kids were always dressed with a bandana over their eyes and spun at least three times in a circle, which was tradition.

My father would tie the *piñata* to a rope hanging from the tallest tree in the yard and then climb to the roof of our house to dangle and sway the piñata for each participant. The crowd would stand around in a circle surrounding the paper maché creature, waiting for the treats to spill out. Sometimes our hitting stick was a baseball bat, a broom, or my baton decorated with streamers. Once the *piñata* starts loosing limbs, children and parents collected the pieces to fill them with candy. It was like getting the flower from the birthday cake, it's always an honor. At some point during the evening, an adult needed to take a hit in order to crack the piñata open. That's when the silliness would begin. All the children would be laughing and waiting for the candy to topple over us. It always did, and we all crawled on the ground and grabbed anything in sight. Sometimes we found apples and oranges as fillers, which would always end up in our fruit bowl the next day.

The evenings would always come to an end after "*Las Mañanitas*"[31] and "Happy Birthday" were sung consecutively. To this day, it doesn't feel like my birthday until someone sings "*Las Mañanitas*."

[30] *Friends and family.*

[31] *A traditional Mexican Spanish song, which is sung for a person's birthday.*

Las Niñas

It usually occurred earlier in the morning when *Abuela* Cata[32] made it a point to be the first to wish me a *"Feliz Cumpleaños."*[33]

Soon after the *piñata*, our birthday cake would be sliced up and dispersed to our guests. My side of the cake always had white cake with pineapple filling and Suzanne insisted on chocolate cake with strawberry filling. The opening of presents followed the cake. The crowds always chanted "oohs" and "ahas" for every gift. As the goodbyes and *muchas gracias* were being said, my mother packed "to go" plates of cake and food. Somehow we always managed to eat leftovers for two days.

Now I spend my birthdays surrounded by friends and traveling. My parents have taught me to celebrate my life. I have indulged myself in the past with wine, bike rides through Mexico, Jazzfest in New Orleans, pearls and this year I plan to be rafting down a river in California with some of my best friends. *La gran fiesta* never ends; this is one tradition I have learned to perfect. Except now I take pride in celebrating my life every day. Gracias a mis padres por esta maravillosa vida![34]

---

[32] *Grandma Cata; Cata is a nick name for Catalina.*

[33] *Happy Birthday.*

[34] *I thank my parents for this wonderful life.*

Chapter Sixteen

Noé, my first love.

Most of my crushes during middle school were developed around the boys my best friend Annie was dating. I have to say the only reason I can remember falling for these boys was because Annie had very strict parents and could not communicate with them by phone or at school. To make matters worse, her mother worked at our school as the principal's secretary. I am not sure how Annie established her relationships, but somehow I always ended up as the "go between" for phone calls and love letters. Many times we would have three way phone calls just so they could chat outside of the classroom. With time, this dating method led to one of the boys actually taking interest in me. Unfortunately, it happened to be the most rebellious one of the group.

Noé was my first love. I am sure there are many stories that I could share, but there is only one significant memory that caused my entire family grief. After a couple of months, Noé and I started holding hands in public. I was in eighth grade, and we no longer attended St. Joseph's together. We didn't start dating until I left St. Joseph's. Our families tried to be supportive by allowing us to visit each other under their supervision. Looking back now, it was a very generous, but foolish act as parents. We were definitely too young and way too curious through our pubescent years.

On one particular evening over our Christmas break from school, I was babysitting for my aunt and uncle while my family went to Tijuana. I returned home the following afternoon but no one was home. I had expected my family to return by dusk. I was on the phone with Noé most of the day, just talking about anything, everything, or sometimes nothing. Most of the time, we would just watch our own TVs and not say a word. Towards the evening, we both started to wonder how long it would be until my family got home. Nine o'clock had passed, and I was starting to get scared of being by myself in such a big house. Noé provided me with some comforting words, but time continued to pass with no word from my parents. By ten, he offered to come over and wait with me. We both knew it would be a bad idea, but it was better than being home alone. We both figured that my parents would probably arrive soon after he got to my house or maybe not at all until the next day. Either way, we would be able to justify or hide that he had been at the house.

Noé and I had shared a very simple relationship. It had taken us two months to hold hands in public and had never kissed. When Noé arrived, we sat nervously on the couch staring at the TV. After a couple of hours, we started to wonder when my parents were coming home. During the conversation, Noé slowly moved in for a kiss. I expected just a peck, but he opened his mouth and I was not sure what to do. All I could think of was pulling away. I think he noticed the shocked look on my face and attempted to kiss me again, this time holding me closer. I did not pull away and allowed anything that came natural. After our tongues touched and caressed each other for what felt like a lifetime to me, he pulled away. The whole experience was a little awkward. I faced the TV and he placed his arm around me, while I leaned against his chest.

I am not sure what was playing on TV at midnight, but soon after we both fell asleep. The next thing I remembered was headlights shining through the living room and waking me up. It was my family's car in the driveway. For some reason great fear was deeply instilled in me, and I think it was because my mind was still a little foggy from sleeping. The original plan of just explaining the situation to my parents was not an option. I quickly hurried Noé into my bedroom and made him hide. After entering the room and locking the door behind me, I pushed Noé under the bed and changed into my pajamas. I jumped into the bed and then realized that if I had my door locked it would be a dead giveaway that I was hiding something. I jumped out of bed to unlock my door just in time for my mother to open it and ask if I was asleep. She asked why my door was closed, and I responded by stating that I was too scared to leave it open when I was by myself. She said goodnight and closed my door. I was quite relieved because I was not sure how Noé would get out if my bedroom door remained open. I lay on the floor next to the bed looking at Noé. He was petrified and kept repeating that he shouldn't be hiding from my parents.

Noé asked me how he would leave, and I told him to go through my window. We had lost all track of time, but later I found out it was close to one o'clock in the morning. As our whispers continued, my closet door flung open and my mother yelled out "¡*Ay, Sarita!*" Noé and I turned towards her in great shock. Noé was confused about why my mother was in my closet, as he was unaware of the secret passage that led from my closet to my sister's closet. I immediately started begging my mother not to tell *Papi*, and Noé kept telling to her that nothing had happened. My mom asked what he was doing here and I explained the entire story. She questioned why we didn't just stay in the living room. Noé stated that he wanted to, but that I was too scared.

As the conversation continued, my father roamed the house to look for my mother. He called out her name in the hallway and she answered from behind my bedroom door. She reached over to lock my door and was contemplating out loud what should be done. She kept repeating that she could not hide this from her husband. Noé and I were both crying in fear. My dad knocked at the door again and tried to open it.

"*¿Por qué está la puerta trancada?* Why is the door locked?" He demanded my mom to open the door. My parents had a discussion about the mysterious car that was parked in front of our house. I think they both came to the conclusion that it had something to do with me, but didn't share it with each other. My father was very impatient because he was left on the other side of the door. My mother held me by my arms.

"*Esto no va a ser fácil para tu Papá, deja la puerta trancada hasta que te digo que la abras, no salgan antes de ese tiempo.* This is not going to be easy for your Father, leave the door locked until I tell you to open it, don't come out before then," she said.

The things we heard after that made us regret the whole entire evening. My father was screaming, asking my mother who was in the bedroom with me. She asked him to walk towards the living room.

"¡*Lo mato si hizo algo con mi hija! No, los mato a los dos*! I will kill him if he did something with my daughter! No, I will kill both of them!" he yelled. "¡*Rafa, es un niño no le puedes hacer nada, ni hicieron nada...me lo contaron todo, déjame explicártelo!* Rafa, he is a boy you can't do anything to him, they didn't do anything...they told me everything, let me explain!" my mother replied. I wanted Noé to leave through the window, but he refused, he said I couldn't handle this on my own.

"I can't let them just get mad at you, I will help

you explain," He said. I am not sure how long it took for my mother to diffuse the situation, but after a while, it became very quiet and my mother knocked on the door to ask us to come out to the living room. We both came out with our eyes swollen and sat on the couch across from my parents. Noé immediately started apologizing.

"*¡El único que va hablar aquí soy yo! Y debes darle las gracias a mi esposa, por ella y por mi hija, que no te doy unos trancazos y te echo a la calle horita mismo.* The only person who is going to talk is me! And you should thank my wife, because of her and my daughter I am not going to give you a couple of punches and throw you out on the street at this moment!" my father said.

My parents proceeded to give us a two-hour lecture while we both stared into the Christmas tree. In the middle of the whole situation they made Noé call his parents. They were also concerned because Noé was driving without a license and he admitted that he had snuck out of the house and taken the car without permission. My father insisted that his parents come and pick him up, but they never answered and after several calls they kept the phone off the hook. At three in the morning, my father stated that we were no longer allowed to visit each other nor talk to each other. Noé pleaded that we only be given a grounding period. My father stated we had two months to gain his trust again, the first month we were to be grounded from contacting each other and the second month would be under special consideration. We had no choice but to thank him.

As Noé walked towards the door, we both started crying. He turned around and apologized again.

"I love you," he said as he walked away. My parents only looked at each other and got up to lock the door as he drove away. My father asked Noé to call our house to let them know he arrived safely. I think my father only did that to take away from the shock of the last comments Noé made. I went directly to my room, locked my door, and cried for the rest of the night. My tears were those of confusion, I was torn between not being able to speak to the boy who loved me and hating my father for being so mean to him. I was also very hurt that I had lost my father's trust for the first time and could only hope that I would be able to face him the next day.

The days that followed were truly a major disruption to our family. My sisters were left at a loss about the yelling that occurred the previous night. They kept asking why *Papi* was so mad. It took my father four days to talk to me again after that night. My mother asked me to be patient and stay out of his way. He was just disappointed and it was very hard for him to deal with me growing up.

I was thirteen years old and only one year younger than my mother was when she met *Papi*.

Not too soon after this incident, my parents announced to us that they were going to separate and *Papi* was going to move out. He passed away in February, before my grounding period was even over.

Chapter Seventeen

Suzanne & Ballet

While attending Catholic school, Suzanne and I also attended a Catholic Ballet Academy. My parents encouraged me to join I was facing my pre-teen years as an overweight child. They thought it would be a good way for me to lose weight before I really started to focus on my appearance. Our practices were held after school, providing our mom with more time to drive across town to pick us up after work. Nini would spend the time at a classmate's home. Since the ballet classes were by donation only, it was an easy alternative to paying more than what we could afford for an after-school program or a sitter.

The ballet group was organized by a former nun from our church and was made up of girls ranging in age from ten to eighteen. Most of them were from the neighboring communities and had similar backgrounds. Mexican-American at-risk adolescents, and by "at-risk," I mean that we were all at-risk of falling in with the wrong crowd or "in-love" with a boy. Ballet was the re-direction that helped a portion of the group through their youthful years.

The ballet company raised funds to take the dancers to live ballet performances to keep them interested. On one occasion, they watched Mikhail Baryshnikov perform on stage. Since then, some of the girls made it to the professional stage, while most of us just fulfilled our parents' hope of keeping out of trouble after school.

Suzanne and I were very eager to attend ballet. We started walking on tiptoes around the house as soon as our parents mentioned it. Once we began our

Las Niñas

classes, I became more self-conscious about my looks than I had ever been before. I don't know why my parents thought I would feel better about myself by wearing a tight, pink leotard. Chuchen was pretty confident in class, and always felt the need to make the other girls laugh.

After several months of attending class, Suzanne's entertainment tactics seemed to wear thin on the rest of the group. On one particular occasion, Suzanne mimicked a farting noise as the class gracefully did repetitions of *pliés*. Few girls laughed, and others turned and gave me a mean look. I turned around and gave Suzanne a *"vas a ver* – just wait and see" gesture, which is usually portrayed with a forward hand movement instead of the side-to-side movement of the beauty pageant wave. On other occasions, Suzanne would start off on *ponte tendu*, pointed toe pose and her, *grande battement*, high kick ended up roughly brushing a classmates tush. After a couple of those, three older dancers advised me to control my sister or they would confront her themselves. I guess the ballet didn't diminish their *barrio* instincts. I warned Chuchen and she calmed down to an extent. Soon after, our ballet recital was scheduled. Between Suzanne's mischief and performing in front of people in a tight leotard, I decided to quit ballet.

Suzanne continued Ballet classes and strived to improve her moves. I blamed sibling rivalry for her distraction during my presence. Little Chuchen was still prancing around the house in tiptoes, but advanced to "toe" (the advance ballet move of actually dancing on your toes while wearing ballet shoes hardened at the tips). Suzanne spent about three years in Ballet, one of them being the year after *Papi* died.

My fondest memory of Suzanne's ballet experience was her first formal event. She was going to see "The Nutcracker," a popular performance that required formal attire. My parents had never attended anything formal with the exception of the occasional wedding and *quinceañera*,[35] so they wanted only the best for their daughter's higher-class gala. Before my mother could have a say in the matter, my father's pride escorted him to the nearest department store to find his *mija* (daughter) a dress.

Suzanne was eleven going on twelve, so her sense in fashion had changed since my father's last shopping experience. *Papi* came home with "*una sorpresa para Chuchen* – A surprise for Suzanne." As he walked in, he urged us to gather in the living room by calling out for each one of us so he could show off his purchases. *Papi* brought home two bags, a rather large one and a second one that was quite small. Suzanne was excited to see her new dress. As *Papi* pulled out his grand purchase, *Mami* and Suzanne stood crouching over his shoulder. Nini and I patiently waited since we weren't really getting anything.

I remember that the bag said Dillard's. The dress was light gray and detailed with pink and white accents. The material was similar to velvet, but the style was what stood out the most. It resembled something Shirley Temple would have worn. The dress had puffy shoulders and at the hips, three white satin ruffles fell above knee length. A baby pink bow was added to one side. Suzanne immediately looked at mom, as if giving her the cue to save her from wearing it, but the surprise did not end there!

Papi pulled matching white and pink tights out of the small bag. Not just ordinary stockings, but the expensive ones for little girls. They had little pink hearts all over them.

[35] *A Mexican tradition similar to the "Sweet Sixteenth," but at the fifteenth birthday. It is meant to symbolize a girl's introduction to society as a woman.*

Suzanne was mortified, but forced a smile to show some appreciation. *Papi* asked Suzanne to try it on to make sure everything fit. Suzanne, *Mami*, and I went into the bedroom to see what could be done.

"Do I have to wear it, Mom?" Suzanne immediately asked as the door closed.

"*Susan, tu Papi escogió tu vestido con mucho orgullo y amor, por favor trata de comprender...pero a lo mejor podemos cambiar las medias.* – Suzanne, your dad chose your dress with lots of pride and love, please try to understand...but maybe we can change out the stockings," mom replied. As soon as she put on the dress, *Mami* and I started giggling and Suzanne a mad look crossed Suzanne's face, but when she looked in the mirror she couldn't help but laugh with us. When Suzanne went out to model the dress for *Papi* and Nini, they both asked about the stockings. *Papi* wondered if they fit, and Nini just really wanted them for herself. *Mami* intervened by stating that she thought they would be too small for Suzanne.

"*¿Y cómo vamos a saber si no se las pone primero?, Estaban en especial y fueron una buen compra* – How will we know if she doesn't put them on first? It's just that they were on sale so it was a good buy," *Papi* responded. Knowing that meant they were probably not returnable, Suzanne went back to her room to try on the pink-hearted tights. With much regret, she came out to show *Papi* that they fit perfectly.

As the evening of the ballet performance approached, Suzanne got dressed in a hurry, tights and all. At the last minute she buried herself in a winter coat that covered the entire dress and most of the pink hearts. As she was getting ready to walk out of the house, *Papi* insisted that he see her in the dress. She removed the coat and *Papi* was all smiles. After seeing his face brighten with pride, I realized that we all would have done the same even if it meant wearing the dress at the age of twenty-one. We would have done anything to make him happy, because after all, he was our proud *Papi* and we were his girls.

Later in the evening when Suzanne returned home and we were getting ready for bed, I had to ask what happened when her friends saw the dress. She said that she was able to hide under her coat for most of the night, until they all went to the restroom together and the bright lights called attention to the pink hearts at the bottom of the coat. Her girlfriends insisted on seeing her dress. I had played this scenario out in mind the moment the dress was pulled out of the bag. As I had predicted, the girls laughed at her outfit, especially at the stockings. Suzanne responded to them with *Papi's* pride and said, "My dad chose it so I had to wear it for him!"

"Can I have the tights?" Nini asked from across the room.

"Yeah, I was going to give them to you anyways, but don't wear them for a while so dad won't think I didn't like them," Suzanne replied.

Not too long ago, I mentioned this story to our mom and she commented by saying, "You know, the three of you are so different and have many different interests. But with all of you I have experienced many great things. Suzanne always took me to the most elegant places, like ballet performances, the Catholic Missions and finally her wedding." Suzanne was the first one to get married and it really caused some heartaches, but not in a negative way. It was merely the fact that we were facing major life changes in our relationship as sisters and they would continue to change after that time. It was hard for all of us to realize we had created lives apart from each other.

Las Niñas

Many times we still referred to ourselves as the girls while we were growing up. Sarah the rebellious one and the demanding older sister, Suzanne the one always striving for attention and vindictive prankster, and Nini the reserved little sister who could be quite blunt when she spoke. The funny part is that we haven't changed much. I recall mentioning at Suzanne's rehearsal dinner that she had done many things in her life to get noticed, so it didn't surprise Nini or I that she got married first just to get mom's attention. Mom was partially right, we are all very different but I think we are the same in our delicate ways. We all depend on each other for support and acceptance more than on anyone else in our lives. Suzanne continues to be funny and attention seeking, but has also embraced many new characteristics that have only enhanced our vision of her. Regardless of the new roles she may obtain, Suzanne will always be Chuchen to us underneath the other accomplishments in her life.

As the maid of honor, I was expected to give a speech at Suzanne's wedding, and I needed Nini at my side to recite the following poem. She read it in English, while I translated in Spanish. I'm sure *Papi* was watching us from above with his proud smile, while *Mami* watched her three little girls through tears of joy.

Sarah Rafael García

"Suzanne...
As delicate as a lily and vibrant like the morning sun.
Each day in your life captured more than a moment in time,
the tears you shed, smiles you shared, and laughter you expressed
touched everyone close to you in heart and spirit.

Your life has taken you from a ballerina to a child's hope for a future,
evolving from a childhood dream to an ambitious fulfillment
leading towards greater accomplishments.

You were first a daughter, a symbol of unified love,
then a sister, a trinity of an unconditional friendship
and now a wife, a beloved companion
bound by an eternal commitment to love, honor and cherish.
Each encounter you embraced with pure sincerity
and led by your devotion to live life as an adventure
inspired by traditions and sacred promises.
Now, as you are defined by these extraordinary steps in life,
you continue to blossom to those who treasure your beauty and love,
reminding us that you are still as delicate as a lily
and vibrant like the morning sun."

Las Niñas

"Suzanne...
Delicada como una flor y brillante como el sol de la mañana.
Cada día en tu vida ha capturado más que un instante en el correr del tiempo.
Las lágrimas que has llorado, las sonrisas que has compartido, y las alegrías que has expresado,
han tocado a todos aquellos cerca de tu corazón y de tu espíritu.

Tu vida te ha llevado de bailarina a ser la esperanza futura de un niño,
evolucionando de sueño inocente hasta un ambicioso propósito
que ha forjado el camino para logros mayores.

Fuiste primero hija, símbolo de amor comprometido,
después hermana, parte de una trinidad de amistad sin condiciones,
y ahora éres esposa, pareja amorosa, comprometida a amar, honrar, y respetar.
Has enfrentado cada prueba en tu vida con la sinceridad más pura,
has tomado cada decisión, guiada por tu devoción a vivir la vida como una aventura inspirada por las tradiciones y promesas sagradas de tus raíces.
Ahora, definida por estos eventos extraordinarios en tu vida,
continúas floreciendo para aquellos que valoramos tu belleza y amor,
recordándonos que todavía éres delicada como una flor
y brillante como el sol de la mañana."

Chapter Eighteen

I hate my life...así puede ser la vida!

As the end of this book approached me, I sat in a crowded Beijing subway complaining about the horrendous experience and how much I hated it. As soon as the thought hit my tongue, I had to laugh because I had never been as happy in my life as I was in those eighteen months. I took back the comment and criticized my lack of appreciation.

I recalled a very sad moment in my life, a moment I had forgotten or maybe subconsciously put away out of shame. As quick as the mind can switch from one thought to the next, I realized I had put away two depressed moments in my life. I couldn't help but recall my first attempt to commit suicide at the age of twelve and then my second plan at the age of fifteen.

I remember being very confused throughout my pre-teen years, and remember many depressed moments as a child. They seemed to revolve around my weight and my mother. Throughout our childhood, my mother appeared to be very depressed, but no one had noticed. I only know this now because one year I decided to make use of all the photos my mother had not used and place them in photo albums for my sisters and me. While going through the photos, I encountered several in which my mother looked so empty and unhappy. At the time, I was living in Miami with her and I had to ask if my assumption was correct. She confessed that for many years, she felt trapped in her life and was just completely unhappy. I showed her the photo and she stared at it with the same reaction I had. She explained the events that had occurred on that particular day. The photo was over fifteen years old and she relived the moment

Las Niñas

as if it was yesterday. In the end, she merely joked about it, threw the photo back at me, and changed the conversation.

As a pre-teen, I had become very depressed and everyone thought it was due to my weight problem. Looking back, it might have been a major contributing factor, but definitely was not the source of suicide thoughts. I still don't know what led to the moment in which I chose to make an attempt. I had very loving parents and adored my little sisters. I guess it could have been the typical teenage issues, like not being in the popular group at school or not having a boy look my way. I used to spend hours in my room just staring into the mirror feeling miserable. Sometimes I would even give myself a ridiculous hairdo and death-like makeup to envision myself dead.

One particular weekend after locking myself up in my room all morning, I decided to make an attempt. As sheltered as I was to the evils of the world, I, for some stupid reason, thought that if I merely stopped breathing I would die. That's exactly what I did. I held my breath until I passed out on my bed. Once I woke up, I couldn't help but feel angry. Not because of the attempt, but because of my lack of ability to complete the task.

I got up, wiped the makeup off my face, and walked out of my room to see what the rest of the household was up to. As the weeks went by, I tried to think of alternative suicide plans since my first attempt was too simple. I guess I thought if it were that easy, there would have been a lot more suicides. Until that day, I had never really heard of anyone trying, yet somehow it popped into my head.

My second attempt was a bit more detailed. It was probably so detailed that it could have been enough to admit me to an institute for suicidal watch. I wrote my plan out in my diary, and I started writing when my father died. It started out as a way to express my feelings, but after awhile it ended up being extended by my imagination. I escaped my world by writing my feelings to the next dimension. I used the sessions to record my innermost thoughts and create a different character. On a good day, I thought I was on top of the world and expressed it by harmoniously recording a ballad or girlish poem. On my bad days, I hated the world and was erroneously angry with God. After my father died, my mother reached out to my uncle Rubén for help. She shipped me away to Austin, Texas for a year. During my stay there, I was reminded of my father on a daily basis. My uncle reminded me of him in so many ways that it was so hard not to want to escape his presence.

My uncle Rubén was my mom's younger brother, and throughout my parents' marriage, he became my father's best friend as well. They picked up each other's characteristics in so many ways. Similarly, my brother-in-law Mario has now taken on that role with Rubén.

Back then, I also was reminded of what I was missing in my life and that's what would make me angry. Even now in my thirties, there are days I feel like I have missed out on a whole other life, as if my father's life would have changed everything for me. I guess it could of, but I will never know. In my darkest moment as a teenager, I perfectly planned out my suicide and wrote it into my journal.

I never expected anyone to read it. The only entity that was supposed to know of such a threat or cry for help, was God. I never expected to actually go through with the plan. Even when I ventured out and pictured it, I couldn't help but envision my sister's and mother's faces of distress, the all too familiar faces I saw the week of my father's death. I could never have done it, out of my love for them. I would never want to cause them such pain, as much I would never want something to happen to them.

Due to my rebellious behavior, my uncle and his wife did not trust me. I later found out that they thought I was doing drugs. The funny thing was that year in Austin was my only sober year as a teenager. I was still dealing with my feelings by writing them out. One day their curiosity got the best of them, and they read my diary. I really don't blame them. Unfortunately, they also read my suicide note. I know it must have caused much pain because I blamed them for my unhappiness, but I think even to this day, that they probably don't know the truth of my intentions. I explained it to them; I had to. They pulled me out of school the day my aunt read my diary. They really thought I would kill myself and felt the need to confront me, but it only made matters worse. I lost trust in the only people I thought I had left to trust. As soon as I could, I returned to my mother's house.

Looking back, I was not easy to deal with. I can't imagine anyone would be after the death of a parent. As miserable as life may have seemed, I have learned to be thankful for the life I do have. Regrettably, my first attempt at suicide was foolish, and my thoughts that followed were disturbing, but now those experiences have helped me appreciate every day that I have. My father's death has helped me live a different life than the one I'd be living if he were still here. Now my goal is for my life to be better than anything I could ever write about.

Sarah Rafael García

Chapter Nineteen

Um, Nydia? Oh, Nini!

I have several stories about Suzanne and me, but Nini seems to be in the shadows of most of them. She is the youngest, whom I think Mom thought was supposed to be a baby boy named Rafael, after our father. My parents had all of our names picked out. I was named after my mom even though she was highly opposed to it, and my mom followed with the "S" theme for Suzanne. Their youngest was supposed to be a boy, so they never thought of another name other than my fathers. When the time came to name their third daughter, our parents considered Rafaela but decided against it because they thought she might have trouble with it growing up. Instead they resorted to the hospital's baby book of names and chose Nydia for its definition, "A place of refuge." I'm assuming that my mother was probably too tired to think of a name on her own after giving birth. I'm not sure how they forgot about the "S" theme, but it obviously was overlooked.

Nini was born on January 4th. Unfortunately, Christmas and New Years have always taken away from her birthday. By January, most people are throwing away Christmas trees and dreading the day the credit card bills roll in, so not many birthday wishes came in for her as a child. For as far back as I can remember, no one has been able to say her name on the first try. That could explain her nickname Nini. Suzanne and I gave her the nickname and we still refer to her as Nini. We had difficulty pronouncing her name as children, but even to this day, most adults have trouble pronouncing it correctly.

Las Niñas

"Um, it's like Lydia but with an N," "No, not Nadia," she always told people.

Nini had other nicknames as well. We all did, but hers have always stood out the most since they are nicknames for her nickname. *Papi* and *Mami* also called her *"flaca," "changa,"* "skinny," and "monkey." She's definitely the skinniest and as a child she was often climbing around everything, kitchen cabinets, couches, and even our rooftop. That helps explains some of her childhood scars too.

Papi used to lift her up and have her wrap her little arms around his neck. Then he would extend his arms out to the sides of him.

"A ver Nini, bájate, como una changuita. Let' see Nini, climb down like a little monkey," he always told her. Nini slowly made her way down. She extended her little arms to each of his arms and grasped his back tightly through his shirt. Once her legs got to his waist, she would use them as a guide by wrapping them around his pants. She took little moves pulling on his attire with her hands and toes, just like a monkey. *Mami* would cringe at each movement while the rest of the audience could not keep their eyes off the entertainment. Once she made it to his waist, she would just slide all the way down until her bottom rested on his shoes.

She actually has a stuffed animal that resembles a monkey. She received it for Christmas one year and was extremely petrified of it. When she opened it, she cried frantically, and it took her days to not cry upon a glance at it. Then out of nowhere, the monkey became her favorite doll. The monkey has survived many trials and tribulations, not to mention moves throughout the years. I don't know how it made it through our household without any major injuries. My Barbies were tormented with unwanted haircuts and even crushed with a hammer by Suzanne at one point, so the monkey was extremely lucky.

We tormented her a lot through the years, but as the cliché serves, "everything happens for a reason" because it only seemed to get her ready for the teasing she would have to endure because of her name.

She was very quiet and observant, and learned faster than Suzanne and I ever did. One afternoon, my father was sitting at the dining room table trying to help Suzanne learn addition by using raisins to illustrate quantities. Somehow the raisins would disappear too fast to add up with Suzanne and me around. Nini watched every tutoring session attentively. Upon switching over to raw beans, my dad asked what two plus two was. Suzanne sat and stared at the table, then looked at Dad.

"Why can't we use the raisins?" she asked.

"*Ay, mija, trata de contar, mira te voy ayudar, one, two, órale ahora tú cuenta,*"[36] Papi sighed.

"*Papi*, can I tell her?" I asked him.

"FOUR!" A shrieking little voice came from under the table. Nini was sitting across from Suzanne at the beginning of the lesson, but at some point had crawled under the table with her own set of beans. No one knew what to say. Nini was close to four years old and had not attended school yet.

Nini continued to maintain her somber state of surprise through the years.

---

[36] "*Oh, daughter, try to count; look I'm going to help you, one, two, Ok now you count.*"

Las Niñas

After *Papi* died, it was very hard on all of us and we often missed each other's cries for help or reaching out as children. I don't recall Nini crying at all until one day in the middle of a normal conversation she just started crying. It had been some months after he passed away, and we had moved to our new home in Rancho Santa Margarita. *Mami* took her outside and they were out there for a long time.

"Why was Nini crying for so long?" I asked when *Mami* came back in.

"She hadn't cried since your dad died, it's hard for her to show her feelings," she replied. Nini has always been a bit more reserved and guarded. She was ridiculed in school for her name, and acquired nicknames there too, like "Nydiot." She hung in there and even stood up for herself enough times that her peers respected her. We continued to torment her at home for being the "white girl" in our family. She ate ketchup with her eggs and only dated white guys.

As the years progressed, she became a loyal friend and reliable pillar to all of us at different times of our lives. Her bean-counting days led her to help my mom through some crucial moments of purchasing a home. She rescued me with her unconditional emotional support through numerous occasions as a rebelling teenager, starving college student, overworked corporate mongrel, and now as an underpaid writer. She experienced her first vacation in a foreign country with Suzanne, then their first trip abroad, and now their first years as married women.

In light of all that she reminds us of, we have yet to identify her as Nydia Castellanos, formerly Nydia García (to our surprise she married another Mexican-American who eats ketchup with his eggs too). In fact, I find myself hesitating to introduce her to people as Nydia, instead of Nini even though she's much older now. People always make fun of me too for introducing her as my little sister since she's almost four inches taller than me and not so little anymore. Nini will always be Nini, *mi hermanita*.[37] Coincidentally, Nini is expecting her first child, the first grandchild for my parents and you will never guess what it's going to be. A baby boy named Rafael. I wonder if they will call him "*chango*" or monkey in English.

[37] *My little sister.*

Chapter Twenty

We all start in Kindergarten...

Kindergarten was where I found that I needed to learn English. Spanish was my first language and I hardly remember any memories in English before the age of five years old. My years in elementary school had some very defined moments, but, now they just feel like dreams that I had in the past.

There were quite a few other children who spoke more Spanish than English and were also first generation Mexican-Americans. We managed to bond immediately. I firmly recall Alma, Petrolino, and David. Alma was a girl in my neighborhood who ended up being my best friend throughout elementary school. Petrolino lived far away and I only saw him at school. David lived around the corner from my house, and I often met him on the way to school and around the neighborhood.

Alma was a slender girl with long black hair. Our parents became friends, and we would share meals together. She also had a younger sister the same age as Nini. María and Nini also became good friends throughout elementary school. Alma's family was very traditional. Her mother was very strict and confined to her immediate surroundings. Unfortunately, she never really assimilated to America and her husband did not push her to do so. Alma's mother never really learned English, never ventured out to work, and never showed any interest in driving a car. They were also very religious. Our family was too, but we managed to still have a balance by hosting barbeques and inviting friends to family celebrations. My mother would join my father for a drink whereas in Alma's family, it was never even an option for her mother.

Although Alma was my best friend for five years, I knew we were very different. The harsh discipline of her parents mixed with other cultural barriers, kept her from establishing relationships with others. Once we drifted apart, I would often see her alone. After my father died, her parents made an effort to visit us in our new home, but it was so awkward for all of us that we never heard from them again afterwards. Many years later, I heard rumors that Alma got married young and María ended up getting pregnant in high school.

Petrolino was quite shy and hardly ever spoke much in elementary school. I think he understood the least amount of English out of all of us. He was my first crush. To this day, I still like guys with similar features—light brown hair, fair skin, and light colored eyes with a distinct Latin look. Through kindergarten and the rest of our elementary years, I stayed close to Peter. He would often come to my defense when other children made a comment about my weight or started a stupid argument, as children tend to do. After many years of not seeing each other, I continued to romanticize about him.

At the age of nineteen, I ran into someone who knew him through high school and could show me where he lived. He eventually went by the English name Peter. He attended a nearby community college, like myself, and only lived about five blocks away from my childhood home, just on the other side of our old elementary school. We got to his house and it took me over a half hour to get the courage to knock on his door. Nevertheless, he wasn't home and I never tried to get a hold of him again. I still wonder what he did with his life.

David spoke the most English out of the three.

We often turned to him for help, but since we were too young to really communicate by conversation, we would just follow whatever he did. We would frequently end up in the "time-out chair" because of it. David was quite an active child and a little too curious at times. My most vivid memory from kindergarten is of him. One day, during recess, he chased me to the back of a small building and we both stopped. I am not sure what we were doing or talking about, but I just remember him showing me his private part and waiting for me to respond. I merely turned around and ran away. After that, I thought he was a little different, but eventually forgot about the incident. I ran into him in middle school and the memory instantly rushed into my head. I could not help but remind him of his particular sign of affection. He denied it for a whole semester, but then one day admitted to it and offered to do it again. I just figured he was being a pervert, but later I found out that he liked me. I was never really interested, but was flattered to know that I was the first girl he showed his "wee wee" to. Over time, I found out he started hanging out with the wrong crowd in our neighborhood and ended up in some trouble.

I bet your wondering where I ended up since I managed to provide an update for my classmates. I had done okay. I even received a trophy for "Student of the Year" in fifth grade. Somewhere between star student and attending a private catholic school, eighth grade happened. I can't remember any major turning points, but I started to rebel against everything and any sign of authority. I'm not sure what triggered those problems. It could have easily been those teenage years, but I strongly believe it had more to do with my parent's having marital problems and my switching out from a private school to a public school. I strongly believe an individual's environment influences their life choices. I strongly disagree it should be used as an excuse to give up and cause major chaos.

I received my first set of bad grades in the fall semester of eighth grade, right after my parents began to have problems and I began to attend the local public school. Once my father reviewed the report card, he furiously ran out of the house and left without saying a word. My mother sent me to my room and chased after him. I remember looking out the window and witnessed *Papi* crying for the first time. My mom tried to console him, but he just shook her off and stormed out of the driveway in his old beat up mustang. Soon after, my father started picking me up from school regularly, although he never mentioned my grades.

About four weeks later, a couple days before he died, I received a three-page letter from him. It described in great detail his struggles in life, including his experience as a new immigrant, poorly paid tree-cutter, working overnight shifts on Christmas, and being passed up for positions because he lacked English skills and a U.S. citizenship. He repeatedly stated that he didn't want me to be a thirty-six year old person, working long hours and driving an old beat up car. He expected us to achieve ten times more out of life then he had, so that our children could achieve ten times more than us.

"*Así debe hacer, los padres tienen que sacrificar su vida para que los hijos tengan la oportunidad de lograr sus ambiciones en la vida…*That's the way it should be, parents need to sacrifice their life so the children have the opportunity to obtain their life ambitions…" he said.

Unfortunately, it took over four years after he died for his words to mean anything to me. My mother relocated us after his death, so we would be able to attend better schools. It also meant we had to live in a predominantly white neighborhood. That experience alone had its own repercussions. I started skipping classes my freshmen year in high school which eventually led to my mom being urged by the impersonal principal to enroll me in an alternative program my sophomore year. That made it more convenient for me to leave school early. I did all my work prior to lunchtime and left for the rest of the day to see my boyfriend in Santa Ana.

My mom soon caught on to this daily routine and sent me away for my junior year to Austin, Texas with my uncle in the military. Within that year, I managed to prove everyone wrong and meet my mother's requirements of obtaining all good grades (nothing lower than a B). Of course that didn't come without raising havoc in my uncle's household. Upon returning to California, I was easily distracted by constant arguments with my mother, alcohol, and the need to see my old boyfriend again. I barely managed to graduate high school in 1992 and moved out of my mother's home by the age of nineteen.

Even while going out with a fake ID and drinking heavily prior to being twenty-one, I still managed to enroll at the local community college and start my path to obtaining a degree. After five years of experimenting with marijuana and alcohol, I decided to quit because somehow all the studying I did on Thursday to make sure I had my weekend free to party, never seemed to get me through the exam on Monday morning. I was working two to three jobs to maintain my apartment, car and insurance payments, as well as tuition. There were semesters when I took classes without even purchasing the required books and lived off of Top Ramen noodles. My closest friends were addicted to crystal meth and I was dating a twenty-four year old guy who persuaded me to leave my chaotic life. Somehow I survived without making any detrimental mistakes or dropping out of college.

Four years later, I joined my family in Texas and was accepted at Southwest Texas State University. It was the only university I applied to because I knew someone that went there, *mi Tía*[38] Iliana. I eventually graduated in 1998 with a degree in Applied Sociology and a minor in Spanish. When I started this book in 2004, I was living in Beijing, China as an English teacher. Now I find myself in the Central Coast Wine Country, checking off more things on my life's ambition list than my father could probably imagine. The things that occurred in between those years is a whole other chapter in my life, so let's finish *Las Niñas*.

[38] *My Aunt.*

Las Niñas

*"Las niñas ya tienen sus propias vidas,
pero nunca dejarán de ser mis niñas..."*

Sara Elba Bustamante

Afterword

Someone once told me that if you think hard enough you can trace your career choice to seven stories back of how you ended up in the given position. In my case, I have probably held more jobs than the average person, but each one has definitely led me to this vocation as a writer. My first attempt to write was in my personal journal that was provided to me by the social worker that met with me the day my father was pronounced dead in the hospital. She gave me a notebook and stated "Nothing I say to you right now will help you deal with your father's loss, so I only hope that when you feel like talking to someone you will, but for now you can start by writing your feelings in this notebook."

Her actions motivated me to take interest in the social work field. Four years later, I volunteered at a low-income clinic as an assistant to the social worker and translator for the nurses. After that, I held several positions, including a parenting class instructor, mental health associate, and social worker for adolescents removed from their homes.

Eventually, I left social work and dabbled in marketing and corporate America. Every position exposed me to more opportunities to write and make a difference of some sort, from social history reports that persuaded the courts to make life altering decisions for youths, to marketing collateral that culminated in project descriptions being published in industry related magazines, web content displayed on the Internet, and mass mailings dispersed internationally.

Now, I sit here in the Central Coast reading my final manuscript, reflecting not only on my childhood but also on my life. One of the biggest inspirations to write *Las Niñas* was the fact that I often heard people comment on my sisters and I, claiming that our bond and accomplishments in life were a result of losing our father at such a young age. I can't help but argue about such comments. It wasn't his loss, but rather the sacrifices and efforts made by my father and mother during our time as a family, which made us who we are today. There are a lot more memories that have made me who I am, but for now I hope the ones shared have provided a glimpse of the lives my sisters and I live.

Initially, my purpose of completing *Las Niñas* was simply to finally accomplish a goal I had set for myself. I found myself scared of submitting to agents and publishers as any other writer would, basically out of fear of rejection. But as everything serves a purpose in my life, so does this book. My motivation to publish *Las Niñas* was one that was instilled in me by my parents. I was told that I am the only one who can create my dreams and then find a way to live them. I am by no means better or worse off than anyone else. I'm just an ordinary person who wants to believe that there is a way for all of us to live our dreams. If one person reads my book and finds it relevant to their experiences, that would fulfill one purpose. I hope that it will motivate several people to believe that they have an opportunity in life. You just need to attempt and know that you have tried and exhausted all the resources available, after all that's what life is, a unique opportunity to live.

Why not live it as my parent's had dreamt it to be for me? Why not live as I have dreamt it to be for myself? As with anything else, there have been enduring experiences and challenges to overcome, now those moments just make me smile and realize that I created my own world to live in and its purpose is solely up to me. Although, I am now an independent woman, I still find myself being a child at heart, living in one of the busiest states in America while making it my permanent outback retreat. In the end, all I can say is, I am happy to know I have never stopped writing my feelings nor have my dreams ceased to entertain me to be my own person. My purpose today is for you, the reader, to find your opportunity and let it guide you to live your life just as you have dreamt it. ¡*Así debe ser la vida!*[39]

[39] *That's the way life should be!*

Glossary

The purpose of the list of Spanish terms is to provide the reader with a basic understanding of the common words being used throughout the book. Hopefully, it will provide you with a general idea of what was used during the childhood of Sarita, Chuchen, and Nini, and in some cases with the next generation to come!

Common Spanish Terms in *Las Niñas*:

Abuela or Abuelita: Grandmother

Abuelo or Abuelito: Grandfather

Amor: Love

Apollo: Support

Chancla: referred to the flip-flop or house slipper that is often used to spank

Chin: abbreviation to Chingado

Chingado: Spanish bad word, for completely messed up (or just bluntly put as F%#$ked!)

Comunión: Communion, as in the Catholic First Communion

Disfrutar: Enjoy

Ellos: Them

Familia: Family

Fe: Faith

Fiesta: Party

Gran: Big or Grand

Hermanitas: Little sisters

Mami: Nickname for mother in Spanish, similar to mommy

Memoria: Memory

Mis: My

Niñas: Girls

Nuestra: Our

Oportunidad: Opportunity

Padres: Parents

Papi: Nickname for father in Spanish, similar to daddy

Perra: Dog (feminine term)

Primas: Cousins

Primera: First

Sobrevivir: Survive

Sueños: Dream

Tías: Aunts

Tío: Uncle

Ultima: Last

Vida: Life

LaVergne, TN USA
26 April 2010
180566LV00002B/4/P